READING SKILLS

THE
WORLD
BOOK

Learning
Library

Volume
2
READING
SKILLS

Published by
World Book, Inc.
a Scott Fetzer company
Chicago

Staff

Publisher
William H. Nault

Editorial

Editor in Chief
Robert O. Zeleny

Executive Editor
Dominic J. Miccolis

Associate Editor
Maureen M. Mostyn

Senior Editor
Michael K. Urban

Writers
Marjorie Eberts
Margaret Gisler

Manuscript Editor
Cynthia Fostle

Production Editor
Elizabeth Ireland

Index Editor
Joyce Goldenstern

Permissions Editor
Janet T. Peterson

Editorial Assistant
Elizabeth Lepkowski

Art

Executive Art Director
William Hammond

Designers
Tessing Design, Inc.

Photography Director
John S. Marshall

Photographers
Don Sala
Jim Ballard

Product Production

Executive Director
Peter Mollman

Manufacturing
Joseph C. La Count, director

Research and Development
Henry Koval, manager

Pre-Press Services
Jerry Stack, director
Randi Park
Sandra Van den Broucke

Proofreaders
Marguerite Hoye, head
Ann Dillon
Esther Johns
Daniel Marotta

Copyright © 1986 by
World Book, Inc.
Merchandise Mart Plaza
Chicago, Illinois 60654

Printed in the United States of America

ISBN 0-7166-3186-5 (Volume 2)
ISBN 0-7166-3184-9 (set)
Library of Congress Catalog No. 86-50558
c/hg

Contents

Acknowledgments

The list of the 100 most frequently used words that appears on page 53 was extracted from information in the following source: *The American Heritage Word Frequency Book* by John B. Carroll, Peter Davies, and Barry Richman.

The three excerpts that appear on pages 70–72 are from *The Ecumene, Story of Humanity* by William H. McNeill, copyright © 1973 by the University of Chicago. Reprinted by permission of the author.

The three stanzas of poetry on the bottom of page 122 are from "The Snow Man" by Wallace Stevens. Copyright 1923 and renewed 1951 by Wallace Stevens. Reprinted from *The Collected Poems of Wallace Stevens* by permission of Alfred A. Knopf, Incorporated, and Faber and Faber Limited.

Introduction

Reading is perhaps the most important skill you learn and develop in school. You read in nearly every class you take, and you need to be a good reader outside school in order to interact with the rest of the world. *Reading Skills* presents simple methods of improving your reading speed and your ability to understand what you read.

Section I shows the relation between yourself and your reading. It explains why you must be a successful reader both in and out of school. The next section helps you determine your current reading level. It measures your reading speed and your ability to comprehend, or understand, what you read.

The third section focuses on improving your reading speed by identifying bad reading habits that slow you down and by offering good reading habits that help increase your rate. You are also taught how to skim and scan reading material. Section IV tells you the many different ways in which you can improve your understanding of what you read. Finding the main idea, remembering details, following sequence, and drawing conclusions are just several of the techniques described that can increase your comprehension.

A strong vocabulary will help you become a better reader. Section V gives some basic pointers on how to increase your vocabulary by taking words apart, using content clues, and making vocabulary cards. The book's final section describes some advanced techniques that help transform you from a good reader into a great reader.

Reading Skills offers you the opportunity to improve your current reading habits, which will help you improve your performance in school. Take advantage of the helpful information contained in this book, for it can help you read faster and with greater understanding and enjoyment.

READING FOR SUCCESS

*This section explains the
importance of reading for school,
for work, and for everyday life.*

Reading for Success

Students learn a lot nowadays from television and radio. They also learn from listening to tapes and records, from pictures in books and magazines, from lectures, and from class discussions. They learn during the normal give-and-take of conversation. But mostly they learn from reading; it is the backbone of their education.

When television became widespread after World War II, some people thought that television would replace reading. They believed that only a few people might still have any reason to read and that television would become the number-one educational tool.

We know now that this prediction was incorrect. There has been no decline in most people's need to read. In fact, surveys show that more books than ever are being sold, and the amount of time that students spend reading is greater now than in the days before television. Unfortunately, however, many students are doing little or no voluntary reading. Most of the reading that they do is assigned by their teachers.

Reading and Your Schoolwork

Just think about how much you read every day in order to complete your schoolwork. How often can you finish an assignment or your homework without doing any reading? Is there any class in school that does not require you to do some reading? Perhaps you do not read in physical education, although students often face written examinations in that course, too. And written examinations must be read before they can be responded to. You have to read in home economics—directions and recipes, if nothing else—in shop and auto mechanics classes, in the science lab, and certainly in such courses as social studies and English. There is no way around the fact that most academic and vocational courses rely heavily on textbooks.

Not too long ago, a group of teachers made a study of students and learning problems in schools around the world. A curious fact came out of this study. The teachers discovered that students who did poorly in subjects such as math or art could still do very well in other subjects. But students who did poorly in reading almost always did poorly in all their other courses.

For a while, the teachers who made the study were puzzled by this. But they soon had an answer to this puzzle. The teachers looked at the subjects that pupils were failing and discovered that even subjects like math and science were based on reading.

Of course, there were also other skills involved, such as learning to add and subtract in math class. But most of the explanations of how to do things had to be read by the students. Many of the homework assignments required students to read long sets of directions. And tests and problems in class often involved story problems, problems that were explained in words and had to be read and understood before they could be solved.

What was true for the students in the study is also true for you. Do you have textbooks for most of your courses? You may use textbooks more in some classes than in others. But for almost any class you will take there will be some items that you will have to read.

Your success or failure in these classes will depend on your ability to read the required materials. The longer you stay in school, the more reading you will have to do. But many schools only teach reading until about the fifth or sixth grade. This means that if you are a poor reader by the time you enter junior high or high school, you are in serious trouble. And the further you proceed in the educational system, the more difficulty you will have.

As you move from grade to grade, your teachers expect you to build your knowledge of each subject area. An important way to build knowledge is through reading books. Along the way, you will probably be asked to write term papers or research papers. A lot of the information you present in such papers will come from reading you do on your own in a wide variety of sources. And finally, if you go to college, almost all your study time will be spent reading. You need more and more information. And most of this information comes from printed materials you have to read.

Even if you could get tapes or movies containing all the information you need to know, they would not be much help. Your normal listening rate is about 150 words per minute. Yet almost anyone can be taught to read twice as fast as that. And you can learn to skim or scan for information at nearly ten times that speed. With the amount of information you have to learn, there is simply not enough time for you to use only audio-visual materials.

Magazines and books may all be on microfilm in the next few years. But they will still have to be read. The same is true of most of what you have to learn in school. Your school is probably not going to throw all printed materials out the window very soon.

Success in school courses still depends on an ability to read. And those students who cannot read, or at least cannot read well enough to master material, are in trouble.

Reading Outside of School

The more specialized the job, the greater the need to read confidently, quickly, and efficiently.

You are moving into a world where every day more and more technical reading is required. Instructions for using appliances are becoming more complex. There are written instructions to follow for food preparation. Traffic signs, travel directions, and safety information all require the ability to read. People in modern societies read hundreds, or even thousands, of words every day.

Also, your ability to get and keep a job is directly related to your ability to read. Even the simplest jobs require some reading ability. And many people advance to more important and better-paying jobs by getting additional knowledge and skills through reading. The more specialized the job, the greater the need to read confidently, quickly, and efficiently. Doctors read professional journals so they can use the latest medical knowledge in treating patients, while pharmacists have to read the prescriptions that doctors write. Lawyers spend their days reading briefs. The number of semiskilled, skilled, and professional occupations that require high reading ability is increasing rapidly. Today, a person who cannot read is almost unemployable.

Yet a recent government study shows that four out of every ten Americans cannot read most government forms. For example, every year millions of Americans give up trying to prepare their income tax returns because they are unable to read the instructions. This is one of many examples of how poor reading ability or the inability to read costs people time, money, and some control over their own lives. Ask yourself this question: "Can I survive on my own in the world outside my school if I am unable to read well?" If you answer this question honestly, you will know that you cannot. Whatever you will have to do to live your life and especially to improve the conditions of your life will involve your ability to read.

What Is Reading?

Reading is understanding the meaning of written or printed words. It is seeing the letters for the word *knife* and knowing that this combination of symbols stands for a tool that you use to spread peanut butter or slice bread. When you read, you are receiving a message that may have been written just for you or may be printed for millions of people.

The reading process begins with the eye. As the reader's eyes move across a page from left to right, they repeatedly stop and then move on. At each stop, the eye transports the symbols it sees directly to the brain, where recognition occurs. The next step is understanding the meaning of what is read. The reader has to recognize the use of words and how they relate to other words. For example, the word *train* has many uses and meanings:

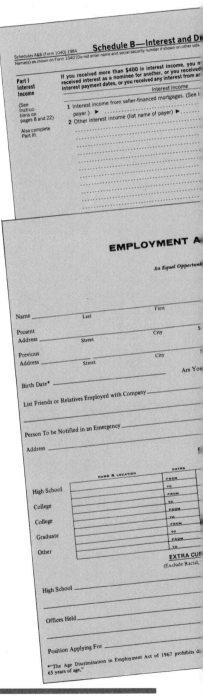

We rode a train to Chicago.
They tried to train their dog to sit up.
The train of the lady's gown was torn.

Not only do good readers recognize and understand what they read, they react to it. They actually have a two-way conversation with the writer. They ask questions about the ideas in articles or stories and question the value of facts and opinions. They ask such questions as "Why did the writer think Yellowstone was the most exciting national park?" or "What is the author's feeling about the importance of going to college?" Good readers may feel agreement, doubt, enjoyment, or sadness as they read. They may reject what they read as impractical or untrue. Often they find beauty and pleasure in a story. The final step in the reading process occurs when the new information is blended with the reader's previous knowledge. Reading a book can change a person's life, provide clear direction for solving a problem, or broaden the reader's interests.

Reading a book can change a person's life, provide clear direction for solving a problem, or broaden the reader's interests.

When you first begin to read, you are mainly concerned with recognizing the printed symbol. You want to recognize basic words like *is, the,* and *saw.* After you master this basic step, you can begin to react to what you read and use what you have learned. Only then can you call yourself a reader.

Different Reading Selections

If you have read this far, you obviously are a reader. And you are meeting many different kinds of selections in your reading at school, at home, and on the job. The way you choose to read each selection depends on what you are trying to find out—in other words, it depends on the purpose of your reading.

What You Read at School

At school, you spend most of your day reading. You have to read textbooks, workbooks, and what is written on the board. You read to check your homework. You read to grade another student's test paper. You can't just write a paper or report for a class; you must read what you have written many times to make all the necessary changes and to proofread the final draft for errors. You read the lunch menu to determine which lunch line to take. You read the daily bulletin to find out what time the basketball game starts, what day the play tryouts are, and who the student of the week is. You read the student handbook to check the rules for absences and for how to make the honor roll.

Most of the reading that you do at school is a study activity in which you are looking for information. Even when you are reading poems, stories, magazine articles, biographies, and novels for your English class or some other class, you are more likely to be reading for information than for pleasure. Imagine how you would read the following lines from the poem "The Eagle" by Lord Tennyson if you were preparing for your English class:

> He clasps the crag with crooked hands;
> Close to the sun in lonely lands,
> Ring'd with the azure world, he stands.
>
> The wrinkled sea beneath him crawls;
> He watches from his mountain walls,
> And like a thunderbolt he falls.

Would you have grasped the beauty of the language or the picture that Lord Tennyson was trying to paint? Or would you have read the lines to find out what their meter and rhyme scheme are in order to answer a question on a worksheet?

What You Read at Home

For most students, the bulk of what they read at home has been assigned during their school day. They think of reading as work and feel it is so closely related to school that they would rather relax and forget all about it. And when students decide to read something other than a textbook, they rarely choose a literary work. It is more likely to be

the latest teen magazine, the comics or sports pages in the newspaper, or a paperback book.

Students may think that they don't read at home because they don't sit down and read books. But they do read. They read television guides, movie schedules, and operating instructions for their stereos, radios, and video recorders.

Few students have discovered the endless hours of pleasure they could enjoy from reading a book just for fun. Books allow readers to experience travel, adventure, romance, and mystery at the turn of a page. Books take their readers on journeys into unknown parts of the world or the universe and let them share the experiences of people throughout history. Reading for fun is so enjoyable that all students should give it a try.

Few students have discovered the endless hours of pleasure they could enjoy from reading a book just for fun.

What You Read on the Job

A person's ability to read has a direct influence not only on educational goals but also on the choice of a career. If you are a slow reader who labors over every sentence, you certainly won't want to be a lawyer, an English teacher, or a librarian—three careers that require considerable reading ability. In addition, good reading habits are a plus in almost every type of work.

No matter what type of job you have right now, some small amount of reading is probably essential. A babysitter has to read instructions that have been left for taking care of the children. A newspaper carrier has to be able to read names and addresses. Clerks in fast-food restaurants must at least be able to read the menu and prices. The student who mows lawns will probably have to read the operator's manual when the machine won't start. And the same thing is true for the student who is using a snow blower.

Improving Your Reading Skills

Since the ability to read is so important, you should work as hard as you can to improve your reading skills. Top-notch reading skills are a wonderful resource that will make your schoolwork easier, allow you to read for fun, and help increase your career abilities.

More important, top performance in reading is going to save you time. You will remember more of what you read the first time you read it. You will be able to decide quickly the best way to read the different kinds of materials you have to read. And you will be able to choose a reading rate that will get the job done most quickly and efficiently.

Since you have been able to read this book, you have the basic reading skills you need to succeed in school and after. But there are probably some areas in which you need practice or improvement. If you practice and use some of the ideas presented in the following sections, you will find that reading can be made to work for you with less frustration and wasted effort. You will draw up your own reading profile that will highlight both your strengths and your weaknesses. You will get a chance to judge how well you read now. And you will be shown how to correct your weaknesses and boost your strengths.

II HOW WELL CAN YOU READ?

This section helps you determine how well you currently read by measuring your reading speed and reading comprehension.

ALICE'S · ADVENTURES · IN · WONDERLAND

Advice from a Caterpillar   if they do, why then they're a kind of serpent, that's all I can say."

This was such a new idea to Alice, that she was quite silent for a minute or two, which gave the Pigeon the opportunity of adding, "You're looking for eggs, I know *that* well enough; and what does it matter to me whether you're a little girl or a serpent?"

"It matters a good deal to *me*," said Alice hastily; "but I'm not looking for eggs, as it happens; and if I was, I don't like them raw."

"Well, be off, then!" said the Pigeon in a sulky tone, as it settled down among the branches, and she had to stop and she remembered that she still held the mushroom in b... very carefully

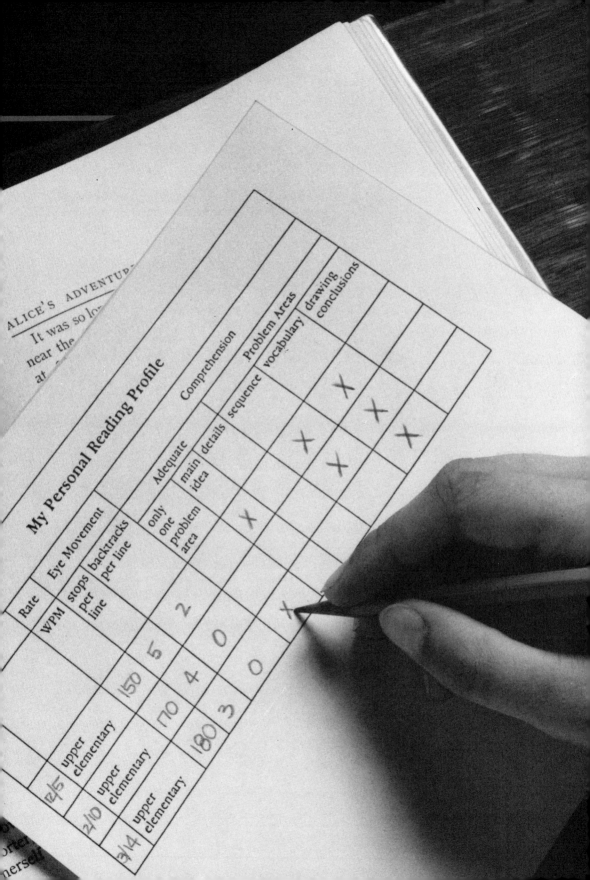

How Well Can You Read?

Y ou probably have a good idea of whether or not you are a good reader. Reading problems send signals, such as poor grades in classes that require heavy reading, complaints about having to read so much, or never reading for pleasure. There are as many kinds of readers—good and bad—as there are people in the world. Are you a reader who zooms through an assignment, then cannot tell what you have read? Are you a slow reader who forgets the beginning of an assignment before you make it to the end? Or are you a reader who needs to make three trips to the refrigerator and five phone calls every time you have a chapter of history to read?

Whatever kind of readers they are, people usually mention two things when talking about their reading ability. One is how fast they can read, or reading rate. The other is how much they can understand, or comprehension. But within these two areas is a great range of other things that makes up reading. You will have the chance to find out what these other things are as you work through the next few sections. And you will have the chance to judge your own skill level on a number of these things.

In fact, this is a good time to try out something for yourself. Why not make a picture of yourself reading? It wouldn't be an actual photograph or drawing, of course, but a written profile or sketch of the things you do well or not so well that make up your whole reading process. Such a profile will help you judge how well you are reading right now. Make your own copy of the personal reading profile shown on the following page.

Store your reading profile in a notebook or in a section of a binder that you already have. You can then use your profile as a guide to setting up a reading improvement program that is just for you. What you work on now

My Personal Reading Profile

Date	Reading Level	Rate	Eye Movement		Comprehension					
		WPM	stops per line	backtracks per line	Adequate	Problem Areas				
					only one problem area	main idea	details	sequence	vocabulary	drawing conclusions

can be the starting point. You can keep track of your progress as you try to improve your reading skills through a program of practice. Just as a doctor measures how you grow by recording your height and weight, you will be able to see how your reading is improving by recording your reading level, rate, and comprehension. You will also discover whether or not you have problems that call for help from an expert.

Discovering Your Reading Level

You can begin to check your present level of reading performance by using the selections that follow to find out how difficult a book you can read easily and fluently. Each selection is about the same topic—television. Each is about 300 words long. And each has been written at a different level of reading difficulty. The first selection is the easiest, the last is the most difficult. Try now to read all three selections at your normal reading speed. Write the words that you do not recognize on a sheet of paper.

The History of Television
(Upper Elementary School Level)

Almost everybody watches TV today. This may seem funny to people who are the same age as your parents or grandparents. That's because TV didn't even start until after they were born or grown up.

Now almost every house has a TV set in it. One-third of all families have two TV sets. More and more people have color sets every day.

All of this started in the 1920's with experiments. They were tried out with all sorts of different machines. Finally, one company decided to put TV's in 150 houses around New York City. They made up programs just for those people. The first one was a cartoon of Felix the Cat. This started in 1936.

The companies had to stop doing these programs after five years. That's because the United States started fighting World War II. The TV companies had to work on other machines that were used in the war instead of just for fun.

Once the war was over, though, TV came back. At first, you could only watch TV if you lived on the East Coast of America. But soon the programs were sent all over the country.

In the 1950's, people got interested in a big way. They would stand on sidewalks to watch TV's in store windows. They would go over to friends' houses to see a show. Sometimes the first family to get a TV was sorry. Their house would be full of friends all day long. They would hardly get to watch the set themselves.

The first color shows were tried in 1953. Almost nobody had a color set. After ten years, lots of people had bought them even though they cost a lot more. Almost all shows are now in color.

Programs on Television
(Junior High School Level)

Programming on television has changed a lot over the years.

The first shows were mostly entertainment. Cartoons, comedy, and variety shows took most of the time. Quiz shows were very popular. They were a little different from the game shows of today because big money went for straight questions and answers. There was a big scandal, though, when people heard that the answers to very hard questions had been given to the winners before the shows.

Public affairs and news programs started early in TV history. The groundwork for this was laid when the first coast-to-coast broadcast showed President Harry Truman beginning the peace treaty meetings with Japan in 1951. The U.S. Senate allowed TV cameras to film its investigations, too. The public was able to see one committee question mobsters about crime. Later, they could see very emotional meetings when one senator, Joe McCarthy, accused thousands of people of being Communists. This kind of coverage was continued in the famous Watergate hearings that investigated President Nixon and his staff.

One thing that many critics point out is that TV has brought a lot of violence into homes. They say that early morning cartoons and nighttime dramas show too many fights and killings. It is true that TV news programs have shown more real-life violence than ever before. For example, millions of Americans saw Jack Ruby shoot the man accused of killing President Kennedy. Millions also saw the war in Vietnam on TV every day. Some people think this should be controlled, but others do not.

One kind of show that has remained popular and almost unchanged since the beginning is the soap opera. Once, soap companies did sponsor them to reach housewives during the day. Now they are popular with many different audiences and have a wide range of sponsors.

Light Splitting in Color TV Cameras
(High School Level)

The color TV camera performs a whole range of complex tasks so that the image before it will reappear before your eyes on a TV set. Most TV transmissions now are in what is termed compatible color. This means that the signals may be received on a color set and result in a color image or they may be translated into a black-and-white image if the receiver is not a color producer.

The spectrum of color is produced by mixing the three primary colors just as an artist does. Yellow and blue mixed result in green, and so forth.

The job of a TV camera begins when its lens captures light from the scene in front of it. It must split this into three images, one for each primary color. Dichronic, or two-color, mirrors are used for this process as blue light is bounced from the first mirror, allowing red and green to continue. Then the red elements are reflected and green is allowed to pass through. The three separate light beams are then processed independently by the camera until your eye reassembles them on the TV screen.

A pattern of electric charges is created by the light striking a target area. As electrons flow from the area, they become the signal to your TV set to show that color in a glowing dot in a tiny area.

Because the signals are separated by color, TV cameras can be made to block out anything that's just one color. This device is used to insert weather maps or scenes from other places. One area in the main scene is painted all blue, for example, then at the desired time all the blue light signals are blocked. A second camera can then fill the "hole" with the desired picture.

Your Reading Level

As you tried to read the three selections, you probably noticed that each was more difficult than the one before it. The most difficult selection that you could read easily and fluently indicates your reading level. It is also the selection in which you could recognize almost every word. For a selection to be at your reading level, there can only be three words that you do not recognize. And you must also be able to understand the information and recall it.

You are now ready to begin your reading profile. Write down the level at which you are reading. The first selection is written at an upper elementary school readability level, the second is at a junior high school level, and the third is at a high school level. If you did not recognize four or more words in the first selection, you are currently reading at the middle elementary level.

How Fast Do You Read?

Once you have found out what your reading level is, you are on your way to finding out how good a reader you are. The next step is to discover your reading rate. To do this, time yourself as you read the following selection at your normal reading speed. Don't hurry or you will not get a very realistic picture of how fast you read.

The easiest way to time yourself is to use a stop watch. If you use a watch or clock with a second hand, write down the times when you start and stop reading. Or you can have someone else keep time for you.

Karate

Even though it took movies and TV shows to bring karate to the American public, it is a very old art.

Karate began around 400 B.C. when religious leaders in India used it as protection against wild animals. From there it spread to Korea, then to Japan and China. This journey took nearly 2,000 years, but its spread to America took only about 25 years. A different kind of fighting—World War II, the Korean War, and the Vietnam War—exposed U.S. soldiers to karate when they were in Asia. They brought it back with them after each of the wars, and many of the schools teaching karate are run by former soldiers.

Karate is the name for unarmed combat which relies on kicks or hits with the hands, elbows, knees, and feet. The name itself is Japanese for "empty hand" since no weapons are used. Students must learn the forms of different kicks and strikes, of course. But they also spend much time on stances, which are correct ways of standing for different purposes. Blocking an opponent's blows is also important.

Students also learn different styles and movements depending on the type their teacher knows. Tae kwon do is the style which comes from Korea. It emphasizes kicks. The kung-fu style, made popular by Bruce Lee movies in the early 1970's, originated in China and demands flowing, circular movements instead of the hard, chopping approach of the other styles. American karate is usually an international mix.

One aspect of karate that is often forgotten is that its purpose is self-defense. Since blows delivered with full force can kill or cripple, students are trained to control and stop their movements with only fractions of an inch to spare. All competitions rely on the quality of the movements, not hurting or knocking out the opponent.

Figuring Your Speed

Reading speed is measured in words per minute (WPM). Here's how you do it:

1. Write down the amount of time you took to read "Karate." If you used a watch or clock, you will have to figure out your reading time by subtracting your starting time from your stopping time. For example, if you started to read at 7:35 and stopped at 7:37 and 5 seconds, it took you 2 minutes and 5 seconds to read the whole passage.

2. Now change your reading time completely to seconds. To do this, multiply the number of minutes by 60. Then add the extra seconds to that number. Using the time of 2 minutes and 5 seconds from the example, you get $2 \times 60 + 5 = 125$. So it took a total of 125 seconds to read the passage.

3. You want to know how many words per second you read. There are 300 words in "Karate." If you take the time of 125 seconds and divide it into 300 words, you get 2 2/5 words per second.

4. Now, change the words per second to words per minute by multiplying by 60. The figure 2 2/5 words per second multiplied by 60 is 144 words per minute.

Use your own time and go through the same steps. The formula is:

$$\frac{\text{number of words read}}{\text{time in seconds}} \times 60 = \text{WPM}$$

An example of the use of the formula to find a WPM rate would be:

$$\frac{300 \text{ (words)}}{60 \text{ (seconds)}} \times 60 = 300 \text{ WPM}$$

To get the most help, you should check your reading speed frequently, using a variety of materials. The easiest way to do this is to use an automatic timer set for one minute. If you mark the spot where you are after one minute, you can just count the words up to this mark to find out the number of words you read in a minute.

For most students, a reading rate of 200 to 300 words per minute is normal. A student might fall to half that if the content is technical or difficult. On the other end of the scale, a student might speed up to 350 to 600 words per minute when reading a newspaper or magazine and up to 1,000 words per minute if he or she is skimming a novel. When doing a school assignment, a student must allot time according to the type of material to be read.

Judging Your Eye Movement

Your reading rate is related to the way your eyes move across the printed page.

Your reading rate is related to the way your eyes move across the printed page. They do not sweep smoothly across a page but stop, then go on, stop again, and so on. Your eyes probably make one or more stops on each line of print. In fact, 90 per cent of your reading time is spent with your eyes not moving. What your eyes are doing at each stop is reading one word or more. The faster you read, the fewer the number of stops you make on a line. The eyes of slow readers move slowly along a page, picking up one word at a time. Sometimes, their eyes even go back over the same words that they have already read.

By using a friend, a mirror, and a book, you can find out exactly how many stops your eyes make as you read. Choose a book that is easy for you to read. Put a mirror on one of the pages, and then read the opposite page. Have your friend stand behind you and count the number of stops your eyes make in ten lines of reading. It takes a little practice to count the number of stops accurately. Write this information on your reading profile sheet.

'If you don't have someone to help you take this test right now, you can get a good idea of how many stops your eyes make by reading the next three paragraphs. The paragraph that is most comfortable for you to read is the one that best describes the movement of your eyes.

Slow Word-by-Word Reader

Moving / from / word / to / word / tires / the / eyes, / yet / many / people / read / this / way. / By / the / time / the / reader / reaches / the / end / of / a / sentence, / the / open-/ ing / words / have / been / forgotten.

The Average Reader

Moving / from word / to word / tires / the eyes, / yet / many/ people / read / this way. / By the time / the reader / reaches/ the end / of a sentence, / the opening words / have been/ forgotten.

The Good Reader

Moving from word to word/ tires the eyes, / yet many peo-/ ple read this way. / By the time the reader / reaches the/ end of a sentence, / the opening words have been forgot-/ ten.

Now that you know a little more about how your eyes move while you read, add this information to your reading profile. Write down either the style of your eye movement or the average number of stops you make in a line. You can get this figure by dividing the average number of words per line by the average number of stops you made per line.

Another piece of information that you should add to your profile is the number of times your eyes go back over material that you have already read. To find out this number, you will again have to use a friend and a mirror. Have the friend look in the mirror as before and count the number of times your eyes backtrack as you read ten lines. Divide this number by 10 to find out how many times you backtracked in one line.

Making too many stops on a line and backtracking frequently are symptoms that you are not reading as well as you should. However, you can forget about how your eyes move if your rate and comprehension are acceptable.

How Well Do You Understand?

The last step in completing your reading profile is to use the selections that follow to find out how well you understand what you read. You can test your comprehension by reading the selection that is on your reading level. The first selection is written at an elementary school level. Read it if your level is upper elementary or lower. The second selection is on the junior high level, and the third is on the high school level. All the selections deal with the topic of resources and are followed by five questions that you are to answer.

These questions will give you an idea of your own special strengths and weaknesses in comprehension. Each tests a different area of comprehension. Question 1 always tests the ability to identify the main idea in the selection. Question 2 is about details. Question 3 is a sequence question and 4 is a vocabulary question. The last question deals with your ability to draw conclusions.

It is not as easy to measure your comprehension as it is to do the math that shows your reading rate. Nevertheless, the questions that follow each selection will give you an idea of how much you understood. If you can answer four of the five questions easily, your level of comprehension is adequate for your reading level. The answers are found at the end of the section.

Natural Resources
(Elementary School Level)

People all over the world live in different environments. In some places it's usually warm. In other places it is usually cold. In many places there are cold and warm seasons. Some areas have wet and dry seasons. Some areas are always wet.

Some areas have many different resources. In some places there are few resources. People use their resources to supply their needs. They trade their extra resources for things they need and want. Sometimes the environment changes when resources are used or increased. An example of this is water.

In dry areas, people may find ways to add water to the topsoil. They make the soil good for growing food plants. They can then raise crops for themselves and for animals. They may use irrigation. Irrigation is bringing water to the fields. Water can be pumped up from far under the ground. Ditches can be dug to run water from far away. Tanks of water can be brought to the fields and pumped out through pipes and sprinklers.

When people in a place are able to grow more of their own food, they do not need to trade for food with other places. They may, however, want to trade with other places for different kinds of foods.

Many years ago, most people ate only the foods that were found in their environment. Now, people eat foods from almost everywhere in the world. In fact, in some environments, such as in large cities, very little food is grown or raised.

1. What is this story mainly about?
2. What is one way water is brought to fields?
3. Does the story discuss environment or natural resources first?
4. What does the word *irrigation* mean in this story?
5. Why are people able to eat so many different foods nowadays?

Water Resources
(Junior High School Level)

Government officials warn that one of the most serious long-range problems now facing the nation is the shortage of water. It is the belief of many people who have been studying our shrinking supply of water that by the beginning of the 21st century, water shortages will affect almost every section of the country. The only way to avoid this kind of disaster is for the nation to recognize that waste and mistreatment of water must stop.

In the Southwest, rapidly growing cities are demanding more and more water. In order to get it, proposals have been made to divert water from rivers. This is meeting with opposition from the rural areas where fewer people live, but where water is used for crops.

In many parts of the country, pollution has greatly affected the quality of water. Underground reservoirs are being polluted by chemicals from various sources.

In some areas even the rain is polluted. Air pollutants mix with moisture and result in acid rain.

Water shortages are often the result of natural events. During a drought, the amount of rainfall over an area decreases below normal levels for weeks, months, or even years. When this happens, water supplies in reservoirs and water levels in rivers and lakes fall drastically.

1. What is this story mainly about?
2. What is one way that water is being polluted?
3. Does the selection first talk about acid rain or pollution?
4. What does the term *divert* mean?
5. What is the only way for the nation to avoid a serious shortage of water?

The Economic Resources of China
(High School Level)

China has one of the world's largest economies. Still, economists consider it a developing country because the value of what each person produces is so low and only about 10 per cent of all the workers are employed in industry. The country itself can be divided into six economic regions.

1. Northeast China is China's major industrial area and the foremost center of heavy industry. This region is the largest producer of coal, iron, steel, and petroleum.
2. North China ranks third in total industrial production. The development of the region has been aided by plentiful supplies of local coal and a relatively good railroad network.
3. East China, though smallest in area, has nearly a third of China's population. Much of the region's productive capacity is located in Shanghai, China's largest industrial and commercial metropolis.
4. Central-South China ranks second after the East in population, and is China's largest producer of tractors and refined sugar. This region is an important producer of raw materials, particularly nonferrous metals.
5. Southwest China, the formerly isolated provinces, has experienced a modified and diversified industrial build-up since 1949. Mining is important.

6. Northwest China, by far the largest region, is the least industrialized. Soviet assistance in the industrial development of the region has been considerable.

1. What is the main topic of this selection?
2. What per cent of the Chinese people work in factories today?
3. Are the industrialized or nonindustrialized regions discussed first?
4. What is the meaning of the word *metropolis*?
5. Why do you think goods from China can be exported and sold so cheaply in other countries?

To complete your profile, check your answers against the answer key that appears at the end of this section. Then record the areas where you are having problems understanding what you read. Study the following sample profile. Note how your profile can show that your basic reading skills are improving.

My Personal Reading Profile										
Date	Reading Level	Rate	Eye Movement		Comprehension					
		WPM	stops per line	backtracks per line	Adequate	Problem Areas				
					only one problem area	main idea	details	sequence	vocabulary	drawing conclusions
12/5	upper elementary	150	5	2		x		x	x	
2/10	upper elementary	170	4	0				x	x	
3/14	upper elementary	180	3	0	x				x	

More About Your Reading Habits

Improvement in your reading level, rate, and comprehension is closely tied to the identification and improvement of your reading habits. As you answer the following questions about your habits, think about how you read the selections in this section. You are the only one who can tell how good or how poor your reading habits are.

1. Do you really understand what you read? Do you get the feeling that your eyes are moving over the words but that nothing is making sense? Do you almost always get one kind of question right or wrong?

    If you are able to answer four out of five questions for a given level, you probably comprehend most things written at that level. But this does not mean that you are comprehending as well as you could. You should still work to learn new ways to improve your reading comprehension.

2. Do you change your WPM rate as you switch from one kind of material to another? Have you ever noticed that you slow down when you come to a new or hard part in your reading? Or do you always read at the same rate?

    It might surprise you to know that the fastest readers are not always the best readers. Neither are the slowest. The best readers are the people who can change speed to suit the difficulty of the material they are reading.

    No one agrees on what the perfect WPM rate is. But people can read easy or light material at 600 words or more per minute and still understand most of what they read. The more usual rate is between 200 and 300 words per minute. Most high school and college students read at about 200 words per minute for material that is written at an average or middle level. Even the best readers should and do slow down to 100 words per minute or less when they are studying very difficult material.

    What you have to do is gain the ability to choose a rate that is fast enough to get you through your reading quickly but slow enough to let you understand as much as you need to. Reading at 800 words a minute does you no good if you have to reread passages to comprehend them.

It might surprise you to know that the fastest readers are not always the best readers. Neither are the slowest.

3. Are you reading out loud to yourself?

    Many people whisper words under their breath as they read. Other people move their lips for some or all of the words they come to. Some people also notice that they somehow "hear" each word inside their head as they go along. Some experts say we all do this. But good readers hardly do it at all.

4. Do you find yourself rereading often?

    Some students have fallen into the habit of rereading groups of two or three sentences as they work through a passage. They keep losing their place or forgetting the content of the passage. If you do this, you are wasting valuable time.

    Even though you will want to vary your WPM rate, you should also try to set a smooth pace. Rereading is a hard habit to break. But in the long run such rereading is a waste of time.

5. Are you reading word by word?

    Anyone who looks at each word separately is reading much too slowly. If you are doing this, you are probably also hurting your comprehension.

    Reading in phrases or in groups of words helps you in two ways. First, you can read much more quickly because with practice you can learn to see groups of words as quickly as you can see one word. And second, you will help your comprehension because word groups often contain more precise meanings than single words can.

6. What do you do when you come to unfamiliar words?

    There will always be times when you have to stop reading and think about the meaning of a word. But if that happens to you a lot, you need to change some of your reading habits. When you have to stop too often, you lose your train of thought. Your comprehension of the content begins to fall. And your WPM rate also begins to suffer.

7. At what time of day and in what kinds of physical surroundings do you do most of your reading?

    Many of your reading difficulties can be solved

by choosing the best conditions to read in. You have probably been told that it is a mistake to try to read while watching TV or listening to a radio. But you probably try to do it anyway. Almost everyone does, but few students really read better with such distractions. Some students can read with great comprehension propped up in bed or stretched out sunbathing. But most cannot. It is better to set aside a quiet spot for your reading—one that is not a sleeping or a play area. Neither is it a good idea to wait until you are tired to read. And reading in dim light is not only bad for your eyesight, it also tends to make you sleepy.

8. Do your eyes get tired or blurry as you read?

   If it has been some time since your last eye test, your eyes could be signaling that you have some problem. You may find that your eyes itch or you may begin to have trouble focusing. Eye conditions can change more quickly than you realize. And such conditions can be the cause of reading problems.

9. How often do you read? Do you read something every day? How much time do you spend reading daily?

   If you hardly read at all, it is unlikely that you will ever be a good reader. As with other things, you have to practice if you want to be good at reading. Your efforts will be rewarded by a gradually increasing reading level and rate and a rising level of comprehension.

As with other things, you have to practice if you want to be good at reading.

Using Your Profile and Habits Check List

Your picture is finished. You have described in some detail how well you read at the present time. If you seem to have a serious reading problem, be sure to take advantage of any help your school has to offer. If you are a good reader—which basically means that you are able to understand what you read—you must keep up your good reading habits. If you are a so-so reader—which probably describes most readers—and, if you are able to get along but little more, there is room for improvement. The remaining sections in this book will help you to help yourself.

Answers

Natural Resources

1. use of resources (main idea)
2. pumped from underground, by ditch, in tanks (details)
3. environment (sequence)
4. bringing water to the fields (vocabulary)
5. They can get food from everywhere in the world. (drawing conclusions)

Water Resources

1. shortage of water in the future (main idea)
2. chemicals (details)
3. pollution (sequence)
4. take (vocabulary)
5. for people to stop wasting water (drawing conclusions)

The Economic Resources of China

1. the economy of China (main idea)
2. 10 per cent (details)
3. industrialized (sequence)
4. city (vocabulary)
5. The value of what each person produces is low. (drawing conclusions)

III IMPROVING YOUR READING RATE

This section points out some bad reading habits that might be slowing you down, and it gives tips on how you can improve your reading rate.

Theme and Variations

242

All in all there are nearly a thousand species of bats. They have made homes for themselves and found sufficient food in all but the very coldest parts of the world. The connection between them and the tupaia pattern is not difficult to credit when you look at them closely. They must be reckoned one of the most successful of the early insectivore variations.

Whales and dolphins, of course, are also warm-blooded, milk-producing mammals and they too have a long ancestry, with fossils dating back to the beginning of the great radiation of the mammals thirty million years ago. But could these immense animals really be descended from little insectivores. But could these immense animals really be descended from little insectivores. But their the logic of the deduction... time when the only... is now so... groups of whales have the sea was... ancestors must have entered the... ancestries, the... ored more directly... nivores and... ly mammals a... The major... become padd... adaptations f... bones burie... have been lost... the time, ha... body to prove... insulator... hallmark of the... comes to... the hairs. So it is o... s, a fe... have lost that too, th... weve... demonstrate that they o... the... ve developed blubber, a... for breathing m... escaping even in th... the problem... als' dependency o... bout n... hale has minimis... clear... paring... outi... an only... bre...

Improving Your Reading Rate

I read OK. It's just that it takes so long." This is a common complaint that students make. Everyone would probably like to be able to read faster. For one thing, advertisements for speed-reading courses make it look so easy. They show people who are hardly able to turn the pages fast enough to keep up with their word per minute (WPM) rate. But it takes you what seems like hours to read just one chapter in your social studies textbook.

As students move into higher grade levels, their need to read seems to increase. They have reading assignments most nights in social studies, science, and literature. In addition, there is the reading that they must do in order to research a term paper, a class project, or a book report. Thus, it is easy to see that having a faster reading rate can save students time and effort.

Almost everyone reads more slowly than his or her potential. How to increase your reading rate is one thing that is seldom taught in school. And tests show that many adults actually read more slowly than they did when they were school age.

Regular practice to increase reading speed will work for most students. The real problem most students have with their reading rate is that they never try to improve it.

Most educational systems do not teach reading skills after elementary school. And yet growth in reading skills is really necessary for older students. It is also true that you cannot work on increasing your reading rate unless you already are a pretty skillful reader. This means that junior high or high school is the time and place to work on your WPM rate. Yet very few schools offer students the chance to do this. And most students feel they do not have the skill to increase their WPM rate on their own.

Habits That Slow You Down

Study the following list of things that slow people down when they read:

reading aloud

finger pointing

head moving

word-by-word reading

moving from line to line

backtracking

analyzing too much

not recognizing words

having too small a sight vocabulary

You may find that some of the habits on this list are ones you wrote down in your reading profile or discovered on the check list as things you need to improve. In this section, you will get some suggestions on how to eliminate the habits that may be slowing you down.

After you have had a chance to try some of these suggestions, you will be given a plan for increasing your WPM rate through practice. Remember, though, the habits on the list usually make it difficult to increase your WPM rate. So you will need to get rid of any of those habits you might have before you can train to increase your rate.

Reading Aloud to Yourself

One habit that really slows you down is going through the motions of reading orally as you read silently. In some cases, students move their lips for each word. In others, they say words to themselves without lip movement. In either case, the student can read no faster than he or she normally speaks—at best, just a little quicker than a hundred words a minute. This is a terribly inefficient way to read.

One habit that really slows you down is going through the motions of reading orally as you read silently.

Check to see if your lips move by holding your finger over your mouth as you read the rest of this paragraph. Even if your lips don't move, though, you may still be reading aloud to yourself. As you read the next paragraph, place your fingers against your throat. Even if your lips are tightly sealed, slight movement of the tongue and throat will betray if you are reading aloud to yourself. This is more likely to be your problem than actually moving your lips. Lip movement is more common in the early elementary grades.

The habit of reading aloud to yourself will not disappear unless you apply real effort. It's a matter of self-training and self-discipline. If you are actually moving your lips, you can correct this fault by reading with a pencil or pen held tightly between your lips. The pencil will fall if you begin to move your lips. If you aren't actually moving your lips but are still saying the words, try chewing gum or sucking on hard candy as you read. This interferes with your ability to move your tongue and throat to form words silently.

The habit of reading aloud is not easy to break. You will probably need to practice for many weeks. However, if reading aloud to yourself is the main reason that you are reading slowly, your reading rate will improve quickly as you begin to conquer this bad habit.

Finger Pointing

Finger pointing tends to make you slow down and pay too much attention to each word.

Finger pointing helps you keep your place. And if this is the reason you run your finger under every word that you read, it is not necessarily a bad habit. Nevertheless, finger pointing does tend to make you slow down and pay too much attention to each word. Finger pointers are usually word-by-word readers. Breaking this habit is quite easy. Simply use a plain 3-inch by 5-inch card to keep your place as you read.

Head Moving

Teachers often get upset when they see students moving their heads as they read. But this is one habit that does not really slow your rate much. And it is quite easy to break. Put your reading material on a table or desk. Then, simply rest your elbows on the flat surface and hold your head between your hands. You will become so aware of your head movements that it will be easy to make a conscious effort to hold your head still. One caution—if it seems absolutely impossible for you to read without moving your head, you may have a vision problem.

Word-by-Word Reading

You are a word-by-word reader if you make frequent stops on a line or tend to read individual words instead of word groups. Some students get into this habit because they run their fingers under each line or point to words to keep

They will leap out and fill your house and the houses of your servants and all your people."

Moses told Aaron to wave his rod over the river. Suddenly, the water was full of frogs. There were so many of them, they spilled over the riverbank. Soon they reached Pharaoh's palace and leapt through windows and doors.

Not only did the frogs fill the Pharaoh's house, but they

were gone, he felt safe. He went back on his word. He did not let the Hebrews leave Egypt.

God then said to Moses, "Tell your brother Aaron to touch a handful of dust with his rod." When Aaron did as God commanded, a new plague, a plague of lice, began. All the dust in Egypt became lice. They looked just like little white worms, and they crawled on top of every animal and every Egyptian. Still Pharaoh would not let the Hebrews leave.

But the Lord told Moses what to do next. Early in the morning Moses met Pharaoh at the river. He said to Pharaoh, "The Lord wants you to let the Hebrews go. If you do not, swarms of insects will fill the land. This new plague, the plague of insects, will be on you and your

people, and it will be in your houses. But the insects will not touch the Hebrews. Because the Hebrews will be saved from the insects, you will know Who the Lord is."

The plague of insects came just as Moses said it would. When the Pharaoh saw the insects would not go away, he called for Moses. "All right, you may sacrifice to your God, but you can't go into the wilderness to do it. Sacrifice instead here in Egypt."

"We cannot worship our God here," Moses said. "We must journey into the desert as God told us to do."

"Then go, but do not go far," Pharaoh said.

"God will destroy the insects for you, Pharaoh, so we may leave. I warn you, don't change your mind as before."

God removed the insects from Egypt as Moses had promised. But, when Pharaoh saw that the pests were gone, he refused to let the Hebrews leave. He had lied to Moses once again.

Moses returned to Pharaoh to warn him that God would punish him if he did not stop changing his mind. The day after Moses warned Pharaoh, many animals in Egypt became sick. Soon the cattle, oxen, camels, sheep, and donkeys were dying. But God saved the animals of the Hebrews. Still, Pharaoh was stubborn. He would not let the Hebrews go.

God spoke to Moses again. He said, "You and Aaron pick up handfuls of soot from Pharaoh's furnace. Throw the soot up toward heaven in front of Pharaoh. Then, another plague will begin."

When Moses and Aaron did as God commanded, the dust turned into big red bumps called boils. The boils spread onto Pharaoh's skin and onto the skin of his servants. Soon every living creature of Egypt was covered with painful sores. But Pharaoh would not let the Hebrews go.

Then the Lord said to Moses, "Go again to Pharaoh. Tell

146

147

their place. Others become word-by-word readers because they must spend so much time on each word in order to recognize it. Reading a word at a time hurts you in two ways. First, you cannot read very fast if you spend time on each word. Second, it is hard to make sense of a lot of single words. It is much easier to understand something you read if you automatically put words into idea groups as you go along.

Read the two sentences that follow. Notice that the words in these two sentences have been arranged in different ways.

1. Being able to get a tan and build muscles is part of why city lifeguards want their underpaid jobs.
2. Being able to get a tan and build muscles is part of why city lifeguards want their underpaid jobs.

In the first sentence, your eyes probably had to stop on each word. Maybe you even had to go back a time or two to get the ideas right. You could read the second sentence by stopping your eyes only once for each word group. The first sentence requires three times as many stops as the second. This means it takes you much longer to read sentence number one than it takes you to read sentence number two.

Solving the Problem

To break the habit of word-by-word reading, you must do exercises that force you to read word groups instead of individual words.

To break the habit of word-by-word reading, you must do exercises that force you to read word groups instead of individual words. All of these exercises must be easy for you to read so that you will not spend time trying to recognize the words.

A good way to begin is by reading aloud with someone you know is a good reader. Ask this person to read a sentence aloud, exaggerating how the words would be grouped. Then read the sentence aloud yourself, imitating how the other person grouped the words. After you have done this for several minutes, you can read aloud together. You will automatically use the same word grouping if the other person reads a bit louder than you do. Five minutes of practice a day for a few weeks should get you off to a good start.

Another way to get in the habit of reading word groups is by using flashcards with phrases written on them. Don't study these cards. Instead, have them shown to you as briefly as possible. Another person should put a blank card in front of a flashcard and then slide the blank card so that you see the phrase for only a second. It isn't possible to flash a short phrase faster than you can read it. Use short simple word groups like these on your flashcards:

at the beach

for my friend

in the morning

before school

between you and me

on the road

to the store

after work

until tomorrow

of the house

You need a great deal of practice to get in the habit of reading word groups.

You need a great deal of practice to get in the habit of reading word groups. Ask your reading teacher for exercise materials that have been divided into word groups, or have a good reader divide sentences for you in one of these ways:

> The teacher / is making / a difficult test / for our class.
> The teacher is making a difficult test for our class.

Once you begin to feel comfortable reading words in groups, you should take passages and divide each sentence into word groups yourself. Then you should read the sentences aloud, exaggerating the word groups.

More Practice

If you are finding it hard to break the word-by-word habit, try cutting a story out of a newspaper and using it as an aid. You can also use a magazine with narrow columns of writing. Be sure the material is easy to read. Then tape the story onto a piece of paper and draw a line down the middle, as shown below. Move your eyes down the line and force yourself to read the story without moving your eyes to the right or left. Concentrate on reading the word groups as you move your eyes down the line.

At first, it is usually hard to keep reading this way for very long. So try this exercise only for short periods of time until it becomes easy.

Moving from Line to Line

Some students have trouble getting from the end of one printed line to the beginning of the next. Instead of sweeping their eyes diagonally, they may go back over the first line and then drop down to the next. Or their eyes may make several additional stops as they search for the beginning of the next line. Since this problem doubles a student's reading time, it is fortunate that it can be easily cured.

If your eyes make many stops, you may be having difficulty moving from one line to the next. In that case, you should take the time to do the following exercise. Type a paragraph or more from one of your textbooks. Triple-space your selection and then draw a diagonal line from the end of each line to the beginning of the next. Your paragraph should look like this:

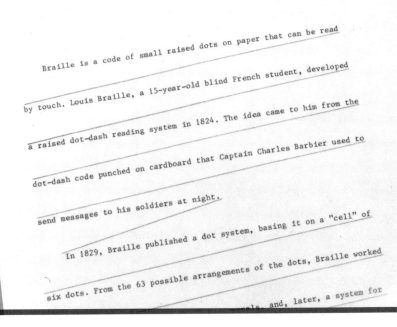

Braille is a code of small raised dots on paper that can be read by touch. Louis Braille, a 15-year-old blind French student, developed a raised dot-dash reading system in 1824. The idea came to him from the dot-dash code punched on cardboard that Captain Charles Barbier used to send messages to his soldiers at night.

In 1829, Braille published a dot system, basing it on a "cell" of six dots. From the 63 possible arrangements of the dots, Braille worked ...als, and, later, a system for

After practicing with several paragraphs that are triple-spaced, work with double-spaced material in the same way. You will not need more than a few days of practice to get in the habit of making a smooth sweep from line to line.

Backtracking

When you read, your eyes are supposed to keep moving forward across a line. Every time they stop and go back to reread a word, you are really slowing your reading rate. You may be doing this because you are a word-by-word reader who forgets what you have just read. Or the material may be very difficult, so you reread it. There is also the possibility that you may have simply acquired the bad habit of backtracking. In any case, there are several things that you can do to stop this habit.

The next time you read, place a 3-inch by 5-inch card at the top of the page and cover each line once you have read it. Cut the card on a slight angle so that it will cover the beginning of a line as you are reading the end. It's a good idea to put a card in every one of your textbooks so you can stop this habit immediately.

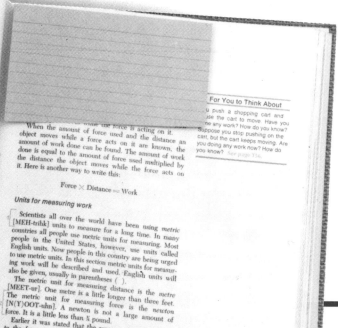

Think again about the kinds of things the students called work. Their teacher said that only one person did work. She meant that only one person did what a scientist would call work. Which person was it?

Mary studied for four hours. Because studying is not a push or a pull, she did not do work. Leroy held a bag of potatoes. He pulled up on the bag to keep gravity from pulling it down, but the bag did not move while he was holding it. So, he did not do any work either. Paul tried to move a cabinet by pushing on it. Even though Paul pushed and pushed and got very tired, he did not do any work because the cabinet did not move.

Anita took the garbage out. To lift and carry, she had to cause pushes and pulls to act on the garbage. Her pushes and pulls caused the garbage to move. Anita did what a scientist would call work.

A good way to explain what work is, then, is to say that work is done when a push or a pull causes an object to move or to change the way it is moving. This includes several things. An object that is not moving may be started moving. An object that is already moving may be made to go faster, to go slower, or to stop. Or, a moving object can be made to move in another direction.

★ Would you do more work pushing open an unlocked door or pushing as hard as you can against a locked door? Explain. See page 758.

Figure 10-1. Riding a bicycle can be a lot of fun. Do you think any work is done riding a bicycle? Explain. Work is done by pushing on the pedals and causing them to move and by pushing on the handlebars and causing them to turn.

When the amount of force used and the distance an object moves while a force acts on it are known, the amount of work done can be found. The amount of work done is equal to the amount of force used multiplied by the distance the object moves while the force acts on it. Here is another way to write this:

Force × Distance = Work

Units for measuring work

Scientists all over the world have been using metric [MEH-trihk] units to measure for a long time. In many countries all people use metric units for measuring. Most people in the United States, however, use units called English units. Now people in this country are being urged to use metric units. In this section metric units for measuring work will be described and used. English units will also be given, usually in parentheses ( ).

The metric unit for measuring distance is the metre [MEET-ur]. One metre is a little longer than three feet. The metric unit for measuring force is the newton [N(Y)OOT-uhn]. A newton is not a large amount of force. It is a little less than ¼ pound.

Earlier it was stated that the amount of work is equal to the force times the distance. For example, suppose you used a force of 23 newtons (about 5 pounds) to lift a bag of sugar. You lifted it a distance of 2 metres.

2. You may wish to show

For You to Think About

u push a shopping cart and use the cart to move. Have you ne any work? How do you know? Suppose you stop pushing on the cart, but the cart keeps moving. Are you doing any work now? How do you know? See page T34.

You can also train your eyes to stop backtracking by doing an exercise that is similar to the one for moving smoothly from line to line. You will have to use your typewriter to prepare this exercise. Evenly space the same letter three or four times across a line. Your page should have ten lines of letters. Then draw diagonals from the end of one line to the beginning of the next. Your page should start something like this:

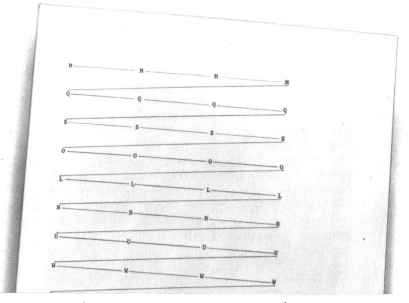

You can use this page to train your eyes to read across each line of letters and then to follow the diagonal back to the start of the next line. You should read the page several times, each time trying to go a little faster. As soon as this becomes easy, you should substitute a simple word for each letter. Then, finally, you should substitute a small group of words for each letter. This exercise will get you in the habit of reading smoothly without backtracking.

If you don't believe that this exercise is helping you stop the problem of backtracking, talk to the reading teacher at your school. There are special machines that hide a word as soon as you have read it so that it is absolutely impossible for your eyes to backtrack.

Analyzing Too Much

Do you sound every letter or break each word into syllables before you read it, whether you know that word or
not? If so, then you are spending too much time analyzing
words. Every time you stop to analyze a word, it will hurt
your speed.

Every time you stop to analyze a word, it will hurt your speed.

To break this habit, you need to practice recognizing
words quickly. And probably the best way to do this is by
using flashcards. Make a series of flashcards for the words
that you find difficult in each of your courses. Then practice reading them after a single quick glance. Or have
someone give them to you using a cover card. After using
flashcards for just a few sessions, you will notice quite a
jump in your reading speed because you will start seeing
words as units rather than as a series of parts.

Not Recognizing Words

Some students read slowly because they analyze each
word. On the other hand, others read slowly because they
don't know how to analyze at all. This makes it difficult for
them to recognize words. If your word-analysis skills are
poor, you will need help from a teacher or tutor. Mean-
while, you can increase your ability to recognize words by
becoming a better word guesser. Just use the first letter or
two of a word you don't recognize plus the rest of the
sentence to figure out what the word is. Note how easy it
would be to guess the missing words in this paragraph:

> The bell rang so Mrs. White went to the d_____.
> She l_____ through the peephole and saw a group of
> masked children. Each child held a trick or t_____ bag.
> Since it was H_____, Mrs. White opened the d_____
> and gave candy to each child.

Having Too Small a Sight Vocabulary

There are certain words that you simply must know. They
appear over and over again in your reading. For example,
just seven words—*the, of, and, a, to, in,* and *is*—make up

25 per cent of the words you read. If you can't instantly read words like these, there are two things you can do to speed up your ability to recognize them. First, you can make flashcards. Here is a list of the 100 most frequently used words:

1. the	26. by	51. them	76. now
2. of	27. one	52. then	77. people
3. and	28. had	53. she	78. my
4. a	29. not	54. many	79. made
5. to	30. but	55. some	80. over
6. in	31. what	56. so	81. did
7. is	32. all	57. these	82. down
8. you	33. were	58. would	83. only
9. that	34. when	59. other	84. way
10. it	35. we	60. into	85. find
11. he	36. there	61. has	86. use
12. for	37. can	62. more	87. may
13. was	38. an	63. her	88. water
14. on	39. your	64. two	89. long
15. are	40. which	65. like	90. little
16. as	41. their	66. him	91. very
17. with	42. said	67. see	92. after
18. they	43. if	68. could	93. words
19. at	44. do	69. no	94. called
20. be	45. will	70. make	95. just
21. this	46. each	71. than	96. where
22. from	47. about	72. first	97. most
23. I	48. how	73. been	98. no
24. have	49. up	74. its	99. get
25. or	50. out	75. who	100. through

You must be able to read these words at a glance. You should not hesitate a second over any one of them.

Besides using flashcards to speed up your word recognition, you can make a device called a tachistoscope that will let you flash a word for just a second. Here's how you do it. Cut a manila folder or some other stiff material in half lengthwise. Then fold one of the halves lengthwise. About an inch from the top of one of the folded sides, cut a window that is approximately 3 inches wide and ¾ of an inch high. Then staple the open sides together along the edge. Now cut the remainder of the folder into strips that are 3 inches wide. Type or print the list of words that you want to study in the center of the strips, leaving an inch between each word. To use your homemade tachistoscope, put a strip of words into the stapled folder and move the strip up or down so you can see one word after another in the window. Don't ever leave a word in the window. Instead, try to read it after seeing it for just a second. As you become more familiar with the words, move the list faster and faster. You may find the tachistoscope easier to use if you staple the word lists together in one long strip.

Training to Increase Your Rate

Once you have eliminated the bad habits that have been slowing down your reading, you can begin training to increase your speed. It is a good idea to put yourself on a training program that is separate from the reading you normally do. You can choose to read just about anything that interests you, but you have to make yourself practice regularly. If you think you cannot do it, you may want to ask for help from your family or promise yourself a reward every time you stick to your plan.

Before you even start, though, review the steps for calculating words per minute. Remember, the formula is:

$$\frac{\text{number of words read}}{\text{time in seconds}} \times 60 = \text{words per minute (WPM)}$$

You should also figure out the average number of words per line and lines per page in what you are reading. That way you can quickly find out how much you've read just by counting the lines or pages.

Choose a book or magazine that is easy and enjoyable. The best choice is usually a light novel or a magazine with narrow columns and not too many pictures. Then transfer your plan to your notebook, along with your information on how many words per line and lines per page you will read on the average.

There are many different plans for building reading speed. Some plans may work better for some students than for others. What follows is a plan that has worked for many students. It is simple to understand and can be followed without special help or equipment. The most important requirement is regular practice. Reading rate does not increase naturally. You must work at it. And as you work on your rate, make sure you always use material that is quite easy for you to read.

1. Decide on a definite time to practice your reading. The start of a regular study session is an excellent time. Then you won't forget to practice.

2. Cut an index card at a slant so that it will cover the beginning of a line when you are reading the end of a line. You will use it to pace yourself down the page. If you have had problems with going back to words or lines you already read or with reading word by word, use of the card can help you with these problems, also.

3. Divide your reading material into sets of a page or two.

4. As you read, you should try to look at the middle of each line or make only two or three stops at the most in each line.

5. Read the first set of pages at your usual pace.

6. Now, concentrate on speeding up. Try to read the next set of pages at a steady but faster pace. Keep your card moving smoothly—and do not expect to recall everything on the page.

7. Pause and be sure you are understanding most of what you have read. Then keep up the pace with only brief stops between your sets of pages.

8. Keep reading for at least ten minutes, longer if you can. You can finish your practice period by reading a couple of pages without pushing yourself so much.

9. Repeat steps 3–8 at every practice session. At the end of each week, figure out your WPM rate for the first set of pages you read. Try to increase your WPM rate from week to week. As you continue with the plan, improvement will be obvious.

10. Add a chart of your progress to your notebook. You can also keep track of how many pages you are

reading each day in the same way. Use graph paper or draw your own lines. A sample of one student's progress might look something like the graph that appears below:

At first, your chart will probably show a ragged line because your rate will rise and fall. In general, however, the rate line should move upward. Your rate will probably freeze at some point and remain there for a little while. This is a normal pattern in building any skill, so don't become discouraged. As you work on increasing your rate, avoid letting your understanding slip. And keep in mind that you have to read more slowly sometimes to be a good flexible reader.

Two Higher Reading Speeds

In addition to reading faster, you should add two kinds of very high speed reading to your total plan. These are called skimming and scanning. They are not what is usually meant by reading. These skills rely on your picking out just a few bits of information that you can use later instead of really reading everything on all pages. Both skills are quite useful and can be learned easily with practice.

Skimming

Skimming is great for a first look at a book to see if it seems interesting or has information you need.

Skimming gives you a general overview. Your eyes move quickly over a page, looking only for highlights, key words and phrases, topic sentences, names, and other important bits of information. Skimming is great for a first look at a book to see if it seems interesting or has information you need. It can help you see if two books are pretty much the same or if they have important differences. It is a big help in reviewing books and notes for a test.

Since your eyes will be flying over the page when you skim, you must know what the purpose of your reading is. Are you trying to find out what a new chapter in a textbook covers before you study it? Are you trying to see what an author's style is? Keep your purpose firmly in mind as you skim. For example, if you are trying to decide whether or not to read a book for a book report, swiftly glance through the table of contents and see if the titles of the chapters interest you. If there isn't a table of contents, glance through the book and look for pictures, sentences, and headings that capture your eye. Note the author's style by reading an occasional paragraph.

Your skimming of a book should tell you right away whether or not you will want to read all of it. If you find nothing that interests you when you skim a book, nine times out of ten you won't find the book very interesting if you decide to read it.

How Do You Skim?

When you skim, you read only a little bit of what is on a page. You have to skip most of the material. If you are trying to get the idea of a chapter, you read only the headings and glance at the pictures and charts. If you are trying to get the general idea of a selection, you skip over the words that are not very important, like *a, an, the, by, to, for,* and so on. Instead, you concentrate on the nouns, adjectives, and verbs that give you the idea of a sentence.

Practice in Skimming

After reading the following selection, see how well you understand it by taking the quiz. Answers appear at the end of the section. All the unimportant words in the selection have been omitted.

Space Stations

_____ space station is _____ large earth satellite designed _____ _____ many persons can live _____ work _____ _____ _____ _____ longer time than they could _____ _____ ordinary spacecraft. _____ provides living quarters _____ carries enough supplies _____ last _____ weeks _____ months _____ _____ time. _____ space station serves _____ _____ scientific laboratory, _____ experiments can be performed _____ data collected _____ _____ stars, _____ sun, solar wind, _____ other subjects.

Russia launched _____ first space station, *Salyut 1,*
_____ 1971. _____ placed several _____ Salyut
stations _____ orbit during _____ 1970's _____
1980's. _____ first U.S. space station, *Skylab 1,* was
launched _____ 1973. _____ reentered _____
earth's atmosphere _____ disintegrated _____ 1979.
Both _____ Salyut _____ Skylab stations were
put _____ orbit _____ unmanned spacecraft.
Manned spacecraft later docked _____ _____ space
stations, then crews _____ entered _____ stations.

1. A space station is a large earth _____
   a. planet.   c. satellite.
   b. starship.   d. rocket.

2. A space station serves as a _____
   a. shuttle.   c. spacecraft.
   b. laboratory.   d. launching pad.

3. The first space station was launched by the _____
   a. Americans.   c. French.
   b. Chinese.   d. Russians.

4. Space stations were first placed in orbit during the

   _____

   a. 1950's.   c. 1970's.
   b. 1960's.   d. 1980's.

Skim through the next selection, omitting the unimportant
words. Then take the quiz to see if you understood what
you read. Answers appear at the end of the section.

The Julian Calendar

The Julian calendar was developed in 46 B.C., after
Julius Caesar asked an astronomer to suggest ways to improve an earlier Roman calendar. Acting on those suggestions, Caesar divided the year into 12 months of 30 or 31
days, except for February, which had 29 days. Every fourth
year, February had 30 days. Caesar also moved the start of
the year from March 1 to January 1. The Roman months
were January, February, Martius, Aprilis, Maius, Junius, July,
August, September, October, November, and December.

The Julian calendar was widely used for more than 1,500 years. It provided for a year that lasted 365¼ days, but was actually about 11 minutes and 14 seconds longer than the solar year. This difference led to a gradual change in the dates on which the seasons began and to the Gregorian calendar, which is used by most people today.

1. The Julian calendar was the idea of _____
   a. Cleopatra.   c. Julius Caesar.
   b. Pope Gregory.   d. Nero.

2. The year was divided into _____
   a. minutes.   c. seasons.
   b. months.   d. seconds.

3. A day was added to February every _____
   a. year.   c. three years.
   b. two years.   d. four years.

4. The Julian calendar was used for _____
   a. 500 years.   c. 2,500 years.
   b. 1,500 years.   d. 5,000 years.

Don't worry if you did not get all the answers right on both quizzes. Skimming does not let you remember everything you read. For one thing, you cannot hold that many words in your memory all at once. For another, you cannot remember something you never saw. And good skimming means skipping over lots of words and sentences.

Scanning

While skimming gives you the overall picture, scanning lets you pick out one thing or just a few facts. Your eyes move very rapidly when you scan. You ignore most of the material on a page as you search for just one or two things. For example, you would use the skill of scanning if you were trying to find a person's name on a list. You have to use scanning every day to read television schedules, the phone book, dictionaries, and indexes. When your teacher asks a question like "What is the Northwest Ordinance?" you scan your textbook for the words *Northwest Ordinance* to find

Your eyes move very rapidly when you scan. You ignore most of the material on a page as you search for just one or two things.

where the answer is. Scanning skills are very helpful if you are doing research and must look through many books to find a few facts.

How to Scan

When you read, your eyes normally move from left to right across the page. When you scan, you must also move your eyes rapidly from the top of the page to the bottom. This is just the opposite of the way you have been trained to read, so it takes practice. To learn to read rapidly down a page, type three words in a column. Look at the center word and try to see the words above and below it without moving your eyes. Give yourself practice with the following series of words:

as	did	work
of	say	find
it	top	most

Of course, scanning is really a combination of reading from top to bottom and from left to right. You read from top to bottom to find what you are looking for. You don't pay any attention to what you are seeing until the fact you are searching for catches your eye. Then you read from left to right to get the information you need. You always have a purpose when you are scanning. You know exactly what you are looking for. Scan the following weather table to find the answers to these questions:

You always have a purpose when you are scanning. You know exactly what you are looking for.

1. What is the maximum temperature in Chicago in January?

2. How many days of precipitation are there in Toronto in January?

3. What is the maximum temperature in St. Louis in July?

4. What is the minimum temperature in Miami in July?

5. How many days of precipitation are there in Indianapolis in July?

Weather Around the United States and Canada

City	January Max.	Min.	Precipitation days	July Max.	Min.	Precipitation days
Atlanta, Ga.	53° F.	36° F.	11	89° F.	70° F.	12
Boston, Mass.	40° F.	20° F.	12	84° F.	60° F.	9
Calgary, Alta.	26° F.	5° F.	7	76° F.	49° F.	10
Chicago, Ill.	33° F.	17° F.	11	75° F.	64° F.	10
Cleveland, O.	36° F.	21° F.	16	85° F.	63° F.	10
Dallas, Tex.	55° F.	36° F.	7	95° F.	76° F.	5
Denver, Colo.	42° F.	16° F.	6	87° F.	58° F.	9
Detroit, Mich.	32° F.	19° F.	13	84° F.	63° F.	9
Halifax, N.S.	32° F.	17° F.	15	74° F.	56° F.	12
Honolulu, Hawaii	77° F.	67° F.	10	82° F.	74° F.	8
Houston, Tex.	61° F.	50° F.	11	88° F.	76° F.	10
Indianapolis, Ind.	37° F.	21° F.	11	88° F.	64° F.	9
Kansas City, Mo.	39° F.	21° F.	9	91° F.	71° F.	5
Las Vegas, Nev.	55° F.	33° F.	3	105° F.	76° F.	3
Los Angeles, Calif.	65° F.	45° F.	6	83° F.	62° F.	1
Miami, Fla.	76° F.	58° F.	7	89° F.	75° F.	16
Milwaukee, Wis.	29° F.	15° F.	11	81° F.	61° F.	10
Minneapolis, Minn.	23° F.	6° F.	9	85° F.	63° F.	10
Montreal, Que.	23° F.	8° F.	13	79° F.	62° F.	13
Nashville, Tenn.	49° F.	31° F.	11	91° F.	69° F.	10
New Orleans, La.	64° F.	48° F.	10	90° F.	76° F.	15
New York, N.Y.	40° F.	26° F.	11	82° F.	67° F.	11
Omaha, Neb.	32° F.	14° F.	7	89° F.	68° F.	9
Ottawa, Ont.	21° F.	3° F.	14	80° F.	58° F.	11
Philadelphia, Pa.	41° F.	25° F.	11	87° F.	66° F.	9
Phoenix, Ariz.	65° F.	35° F.	3	105° F.	75° F.	4
Pittsburgh, Pa.	37° F.	21° F.	16	83° F.	62° F.	11
Regina, Sask.	12° F.	−7° F.	11	81° F.	52° F.	10
St. Louis, Mo.	41° F.	26° F.	8	90° F.	72° F.	9
Salt Lake City, Utah	36° F.	17° F.	10	92° F.	61° F.	4
San Francisco, Calif.	56° F.	40° F.	11	69° F.	52° F.	0
Seattle, Wash.	43° F.	31° F.	19	75° F.	53° F.	5
Toronto, Ont.	31° F.	18° F.	16	81° F.	61° F.	10
Vancouver, B.C.	42° F.	33° F.	19	74° F.	55° F.	6
Washington, D.C.	44° F.	29° F.	10	87° F.	68° F.	10
Winnipeg, Man.	9° F.	−8° F.	12	80° F.	57° F.	10

More Skimming and Scanning Practice

You should probably practice all the skimming and scanning you can when you are studying your textbooks. For example, give yourself the assignment of looking for names and dates in a chapter in your social studies book. Scan the index of a book to see how quickly you can find the page where a homework question might be answered. Skim some of your assignments before you go back to read them closely.

Try to add skimming and scanning to the choices you think about before you begin any reading. You will find that you can use these two techniques for many purposes.

Choosing the Right Rate

Would it surprise you to learn that reading slower should be part of your program to improve your rate? Recall that when you were making your reading profile, one of the questions on the check list asked about reading rate. You were supposed to check if you changed your reading rate as material got more difficult.

Choosing the right rate is the sign of a good reader.

Choosing the right rate is the sign of a good reader. It is also something that takes thinking and practice. In order to choose the right rate you have to have a purpose for reading. Look at the following table of reading rates. How do they compare to the rates that you use for different materials?

Suggested Rates Used for Different Purposes

Words per minute	Purpose
150 or less	hard, very technical, poetic, or unfamiliar material
200–300	normal studying, average material
350–600	light reading, newspapers, magazines
up to 1,000	skimming and scanning

The numbers on this table give you a general idea of how reading rate should vary for different materials. No matter what your reading rate is right now, you can see that it will be too fast for some purposes and too slow for others. What you need to do is to get a sense of what you can do at each different rate. Then you can choose the rate that will be best for each purpose that you have.

The Advantages of Improving Your Rate

Improving your WPM rate allows you to use your reading time more efficiently. And it may also help to make reading more interesting. An improved WPM rate can lead you to enjoy reading more and get more practice out of it. But keep in mind that both a good level of comprehension and a good WPM are necessary for effective reading.

Answers

Space Stations
1. c   3. d
2. b   4. c

The Julian Calendar
1. c   3. d
2. b   4. b

IV IMPROVING YOUR UNDERSTANDING

This section contains many tips on how to improve your reading comprehension.

catalogue under the title of the book or under the author's name. The call number, which is found in the upper left-hand corner of the card, will tell you where the book is located. On the other hand, you are looking for any astronomy book, check the card catalogue under the topic Astronomy. You will find cards that describe books on astronomy available to you.

The Readers' Guide to Periodicals

The Readers' Guide to Periodicals is a subject listing, by subject, of all the articles that appear in magazines every month. The Readers' Guide provides a listing of nonfiction articles. For the most recent listing on a particular topic, check the most recent Readers' Guide.

Files, Film, and Records

Two useful files in the library are the picture file and the vertical file. As its name suggests, the picture file contains pictures of all kinds. The vertical file contains informational material published by various organizations. Both files are arranged alphabetically by subject.

Nowadays, many libraries are installing listening centers, where you will find headphones, cassette tapes, and records. These materials cannot be removed, newspapers,

Library Reference Skills

I. The Dewey Decimal System

II. The Readers' Guide to Periodical Literature.

III. Files, Film, and Records

IV. Special Services

A. Bookmobiles

B. Large Print Books

C. Talking Books

Improving Your Understanding

*I*t is always disturbing to realize that you have *finished an entire page or chapter but do not truly understand what you have read. Failure to understand is the most serious reading problem a student can have. It can actually make reading seem like a waste of time.*

Students don't understand what they read for many of the same reasons that they read slowly. Reading aloud to yourself, word-by-word reading, rereading, and a small vocabulary restrict your comprehension just as they slow your rate. You should have already begun to work on any of these problems that you might have. However, there are lots of other things that can ruin your comprehension, including poor basic comprehension skills and the inability to keep your mind on your reading.

Take a look at the reading profile you started in Section II. Was your comprehension level adequate? Did you have any skill areas that were causing you problems? Were you able to find the main idea, remember details, follow sequence, and draw conclusions? Did you have a good vocabulary? You need all of these skills in order to understand what you read. Having a good vocabulary is so important to both rate and comprehension that all of the next section will be devoted to that subject. In the meantime, this section will focus on ways to improve the other comprehension skills.

Reading with a Purpose in Mind

The first step toward improving your comprehension is to have a purpose in mind. You need to know exactly why you are reading something. Knowing what you want to accomplish increases your chances of succeeding. In fact, you may even want to write down your purpose before you begin reading.

If you are reading for a test that you know will include lots of names and dates, you will need to read slowly and pay close attention to facts and details. If you know that you are going to have an essay test or must write a paper, you will need to look for main ideas. You will note only the more important facts.

Your purpose will be one thing if the story you read is part of a unit in which you are expected to compare certain characters. It will be very different if you know the story is an example of a certain kind of writing and you are supposed to show how it fits into that model.

Other kinds of reading, perhaps in a science or industrial arts course, will require you to identify certain principles and know how to apply them or make them work. When that is true, your purpose again is different.

It matters little what the purpose for doing the reading is. Obviously, the purpose will vary from one situation to another. But it is important that you always have a purpose. A purpose gives you a fixed point to use in organizing information.

When you start to read something, think of everything you need to get out of it. This will help you decide what to emphasize as you read.

Once you know what your purpose is, you can choose the rate that is best for that type of reading. For example, if you are trying to find out about photosynthesis, you will read at your regular studying rate. But if you are searching for the formula for the area of a pyramid, you will scan until you find that particular information. And in order to get acquainted with a new chapter in your health book, you will skim through by reading the headings.

When you start to read something, think of everything you need to get out of it.

Expecting to Succeed

When you are faced with a reading assignment, expect to understand it. Attitude counts for a lot in school. Don't hold yourself back from success by never expecting to understand what you read. Remarks like "I'll never be able to get this" or "The teacher expects the impossible" give you a negative attitude. Instead, the next time you are faced with a difficult reading assignment, tell yourself, "I know that I can understand this." That is the attitude of successful readers.

Finding the Main Idea

In every well-written paragraph, there is one and only one main idea.

Almost everything that you read is made up of paragraphs—textbooks, newspaper articles, magazine stories, and so on. It is rather difficult to think of any reading that doesn't involve paragraphs. And in every well-written paragraph, there is one and only one main idea. All the other details are there to tell more about this one idea. Obviously, if you know what the main idea of each paragraph is, you understand what the author thinks is important.

Authors usually help you find the main idea of each paragraph by writing a topic sentence that tells what it is. Much of the time the topic sentence is very easy to find because it is the first sentence in the paragraph. But you can't depend on that because some authors like to end a paragraph with a topic sentence, and other authors put a topic sentence elsewhere in a paragraph. In order to find a topic sentence, you must get in the habit of asking yourself a couple of questions at the end of every paragraph:

1. What is the one person, place, or thing written about in this paragraph?

2. Why is this person, place, or thing so important that the author has written about it?

Use these two questions to find the main idea in the following paragraph:

> The spread of American food crops was the other great change that transformed the African scene in these centuries. Maize and sweet potatoes became the staples of West African agriculture, and maize spread throughout the continent. The additional food supply thus made available may have permitted population growth so rapid as to make

up for the losses to the slave trade. Although millions of innocent captives were sent to the New World to labor in the plantations of Brazil, the Caribbean, and the southern colonies on the North American mainland, there is no sign of lasting depopulation of African territories.

The topic sentence is the first sentence. All the other sentences just add details. Try to identify the topic sentence in the next paragraph:

> William was a vigorous king, but he was mainly interested in his wars against Louis XIV on the continent. As long as his new kingdom supported such wars, he was well content to leave the government in the hands of ministers agreeable to Parliament. Queen Anne (reigned 1702–1714), George I of Hanover (reigned 1714–1727), and George II (reigned 1727–1760) followed the same policy. They found it simpler to govern when their ministers could get support for their acts in Parliament. Indeed, both the kings, George I and II, did not speak English easily and stayed away from most of the meetings of the ministers at which government policy was discussed. They were satisfied, as a matter of fact, to give the responsibility of choosing ministers to Robert Walpole, an ordinary member of Parliament who was able to win the confidence of both the monarch and of a majority in Parliament. In common speech he came to be called prime minister; and the group of ministers he selected were referred to as the cabinet.

Which sentence is the topic sentence? Is it the first sentence? No. The paragraph tells you nothing about William's vigor or his wars with France. The heart of the matter lies in the second sentence, although you must be careful here. The key lies in the phrase "well content to leave the government in the hands of ministers agreeable to Parliament." The author uses William as a lead-in to his main point, an example of how parliamentary power grew in England. Let's look at another paragraph:

> Britain's internal political development was almost exactly opposite to the French experience. When the Stuart kings first came to the throne in 1603, they tried to build an efficient royal government like the French. This soon got

them into trouble with Parliament, a medieval institution that got in the way of efficient administration by refusing to grant needed taxes and by defending unruly groups that refused to obey the king in matters of religion and taxation. Indeed in 1642, relations between Charles I and Parliament got so bad that civil war broke out. Parliament won, and in 1649 a special commission decided that King Charles should be executed for failing to keep his promises to Parliament. But cutting off Charles's head solved nothing and, in fact, shocked many Englishmen.

Which sentence tells the reader what the paragraph is about? Not the first, nor the second. It's the third because the paragraph is mainly about Charles I's relations with Parliament. Now for a paragraph that has the topic sentence in yet another place:

When I awoke I didn't dress immediately, but ate breakfast first and wrote letters for a couple of hours. Then I dressed and went out, walking for an hour or so along the river bank. Remembering that my food was almost gone, after lunch I visited my favorite store to buy groceries. I then stopped for a cup of coffee, returning home pleasantly tired and in good spirits late in the afternoon. This is how I spent that day.

Where is the topic sentence? At the end, of course.

If you find it hard to pick out the topic sentence in a paragraph, try out the first sentence to see if it summarizes most of the information given. If it doesn't, look at the last sentence for clue words and phrases like *therefore, overall,* and *we can see.*

You can train yourself to spot topic sentences.

You can train yourself to spot topic sentences. Once you find them, your comprehension will increase because you will have points around which to cluster the other sentences and thus organize the meanings of the paragraphs you read.

One caution—some writers, including good ones, don't always include an obvious topic sentence. The paragraph will still contain only one main point, but the writer leaves it up to the reader to discover what that point is. This is not a trick; it is simply the way some authors write.

Remembering Details

When you are reading, it is often just as important to remember details as it is to find the main idea. This is especially true if you are studying, for it is details that let you learn about a subject in depth. It isn't enough to know that Columbus discovered America. You must also know details like dates, the names of his ships, where he first saw land, the problems he had with his crew, and how many voyages he made.

Throughout your life, you will need to read for details. Later on, when you are working, you will probably have to read a great deal of technical material and remember most of the details. For example, teachers, doctors, nurses, engineers, and lawyers all have to remember many details.

The easiest way to remember details is to tie them to the main idea. Look at the following paragraph about yogurt. Can you find the topic sentence and then summarize what the important details were?

> Some dieters rely on yogurt as a low-calorie meal. While it is true that plain yogurt is low in calories and high in protein, many people do not realize that the flavored yogurts can be very fattening. Yogurt has all the nutritional value of milk. While low-fat milk is often used to make yogurt, the flavoring can be high in sugar. And sugar is a substance many people are anxious to keep out of their diet.

The first sentence was the topic sentence. The details are (1) plain yogurt is low in calories, and (2) flavored yogurts can be high in sugar and very fattening.

Perhaps one of the best ways to show how details are related to the main idea is by making an outline. Notice how easy it is to see the relationship among details in the following outline:

I. Some dieters rely on yogurt as a low-calorie meal.
    A. Plain yogurt is low in calories.
    B. Flavored yogurts can be high in sugar and very fattening.

When you own a textbook, you can show the relationship between the main idea and the important details by underlining the topic sentence, circling key details, and then drawing a line from the details to the topic sentence. Using this technique, the paragraph on yogurt would look like this:

> Some dieters rely on yogurt as a low-calorie meal. While it is true that (plain yogurt is low in calories) and high in protein, many people do not realize that the (flavored yogurts can be very fattening.) Yogurt has all the nutritional value of milk. While low-fat milk is often used to make yogurt, the (flavoring can be high in sugar.) And sugar is a substance many people are anxious to keep out of their diet.

Once you have learned how to find details, making note of them will help you to review. Besides outlining or circling the details, you can take brief notes that summarize them in a word or two. You can also make margin notes in your textbook if you own it. For example, you can show where the important details are by putting stars in front of those lines.

Building Skills

1. Why is the diagram a good summary of the selection?
2. List an important point about each of the following that could be included in a summary of the selection.
   a. magma
   b. sedimentary rock
   c. igneous rock
   d. metamorphic rock

Summarizing in Social Studies

The following textbook excerpt is not accompanied by side-notes. Read the selection and look for the kinds of information you would include in a summary. Then answer the questions.

Mixture of old and new

Rapid modernization

Mexico is our nearest neighbor to the south. Every year, thousands of Americans visit Mexico, the only Latin American country which shares a boundary with the United States. These visitors find Mexico a fascinating land of contrasts. They see many reminders of the Aztec and Spanish past, but they also find much in present-day Mexico that resembles our own way of living. Along with villages where people live much as they did in 1500, there are modern bustling cities. Many Mexicans still farm the land or turn out handmade articles as their ancestors did, but others work in factories, in oil fields, and in stores and businesses.

Mexico is rapidly becoming a modern nation. In recent years the government has done a great deal to educate its people, to improve housing, and to promote public health programs. The government has also provided irrigation systems for dry farm lands and has helped farmers

improve their crops. In addition to raising food crops and cattle for their own use, Mexicans grow large amounts of coffee and other tropical products for export. Mexico also grows half the world's supply of sisal, a cactus fiber used for making rope. Mining is important too. Mexico is among the world leaders in silver production, and produces more petroleum than any other Latin American country except Venezuela. Mexican factories supply a variety of goods for its people.

— This Is America's Story
Houghton Mifflin

Building Skills

1. Which of the following would you include in a summary of the first paragraph of the selection?
   a. Mexico is the only Latin American country bordering the United States.
   b. Mexico is a blending of the ancient and the modern.
   c. Every year thousands of Americans visit Mexico.
   d. Mexicans farm the land and also work in factories, oil fields, and stores.
2. Which of the following is the better summary of the second paragraph? Explain your answer.

   Mexico is becoming modern. The government is working to improve education and increase the number of public health programs. Farms are being irrigated, and farmers are receiving government aid for crop improvement.

   The Mexican government is working to improve education, housing, public health, irrigation, and farming. Coffee and sisal are major exports, and Me...

Practice finding details in the following story about atomic clocks. Next, show what the details are by outlining, circling, taking notes, or making margin notes. Then, show that you found the important details by answering the questions at the end of the story.

People have always wanted to know what time it is. They may not have had the mania for clock watching that many people have today. But as far back as the beginning of recorded history people seem to have made use of movement of some kind to mark the passage of time.

Shadows of trees moved as the sun passed through the sky, and so ancient people made sundials to chart that movement. The clepsydra, or water clock, relied on the regular flow of water from one vessel to another to mark the passage of time. Mechanical clocks relied on the movement of gears and wheels to show the changing of minutes and hours.

These clocks all used observable movements as the basis of their timekeeping. Accuracy was good, but not precise. It was only with the advent of the atomic clock that accuracy became almost unbelievable.

The atomic clock is actually tuned to the movement of molecules and atoms. These movements cause vibrations. The vibrations are just a tiny fraction of the movement used in the past to judge the passage of time.

The accuracy of atomic clocks can be set to within a few seconds in 100,000 years. It is rare that such accuracy is needed—certainly we can make do with much greater margins for error in our wrist watches. But for scientific work, where time is measured in the tiniest segments and the smallest change is critical, atomic clocks are necessary.

1. What did ancient people use to mark the passage of time?

2. What is a clepsydra?

3. What kind of movement is used to tune an atomic clock?

4. How accurate can an atomic clock be?

5. Why are atomic clocks necessary?

Following Sequence

What happens first? What happens next? How does it end? This is what is meant by sequence. It is the order of events. Being able to follow the sequence of events in a story is an important part of comprehension. "Cinderella" wouldn't make much sense to you if you didn't understand that she had met her fairy godmother before she met the prince. Nor would "The Three Bears" make any sense if you didn't understand that the three bears had left the house before Goldilocks arrived.

It is not too difficult to understand the sequence of events in most stories. Authors usually tell a story from beginning to end just as it happened. They also use words like *first, next, then, finally,* and *at last* that give you clues to the order of events.

If you have trouble keeping the events in a story in order, there are several things that you can do. You can jot down notes that will help you recall the order in which things happened. You can try to retell a story to a friend. Or you can discuss the story with someone. As you read stories, you should get in the habit of thinking about what is going to happen next. Read the following paragraph. Then decide what the next event will be.

> It is 9 o'clock at night. Tom has just finished writing a report for his history class. He decides to get a glass of milk to drink as he proofreads his report for the final time. Tom sees an error, puts the report and the glass of milk on his desk, and reaches for an eraser. His. . . .

It was easy to guess, wasn't it? Tom's arm will hit the milk and spill it all over his report.

Sequence is important in all the reading you do at school. For example, when doing a lab experiment in science, you have to put chemicals together in the right order to get the correct results. Whenever you have to do anything in a certain order, get in the habit of checking off each step as you complete it. In another course, social studies, you have to know if one event came before or after another. Use time lines to understand dates. Then, for instance, you will see at a glance that the Emancipation Proclamation was issued by Lincoln after the Civil War began.

Drawing Conclusions

In much of your reading, especially in textbooks, you do not need to draw conclusions because the author has summed up the material for you. However, there are times when you must form your own opinion from the facts that are given. When this happens, you have to collect the important details and think about them. If you have taken notes on the details or made an outline of how the details relate to the main idea, your job will be rather easy.

When you draw a conclusion, you make up your mind about something. Can you draw conclusions from the following sets of facts?

1. To win a prize for selling magazines, a student must sell 15 new subscriptions. Rosaline has sold 14 subscriptions. Therefore, . . .

2. Jim must get up by 6:30 to catch the school bus at 7:15. Jim's alarm went off at 7:30 today. It appears that. . . .

3. The school cafeteria always serves pizza on Tuesday. Today is Tuesday. The menu will read. . . .

Following Directions

At school you are frequently required to read and follow directions. You have to read the directions to know how to take a test, do a homework assignment, or complete a page in a workbook correctly. And if you don't read the directions carefully enough, you may flunk a test or have to redo your homework and workbook assignments.

The best way to become an expert at reading directions is simply to read directions. The results you get will usually tell you if you have understood. The video recorder will record the program you wanted. The clock you set will go off at the right time. The cake you made will taste delicious.

Read the directions below to see whether or not you are good at following directions. You will need two pencils and a piece of paper.

1. Put one pencil between your teeth.

2. Keep it there until you are told to remove it.

3. Put the other pencil in your writing hand.

4. Draw a three-inch circle at the bottom of a piece of paper.

5. Draw a triangle on top of the circle that has two-inch sides.

6. Put a one-inch circle on the top of the triangle.

7. Put a dot in the center of the first circle.

8. Draw two dots an inch apart and one inch above the first dot.

9. Draw a one-inch straight line one inch below the first dot.

If you followed the directions carefully, you have drawn a clown with one pencil and you still have the other pencil clenched between your teeth. Take the pencil from between your teeth now.

Finding Out the Author's Plan

You can find out an author's plans by using the clues that he or she gives you.

You need to find out what plan the author had in mind for the material that you are reading. Just as any house that an architect builds goes back to a plan, the printed words that you read go back to a plan that an author had before the first word was ever written. You can discover an author's plans by using the clues that he or she gives you.

Most chapters in textbooks start with an overview and end with a summary. Take the time to read the overview before you begin the chapter. And never put a book away until you have read the summary. You will find other good clues throughout the chapter by reading all the headings and subheadings. Don't overlook all the words that have been written in bold type or italics. Clues can also be found in the notes that are written under charts, graphs, or pictures.

Take the time to read the overview before you begin the chapter. And never put a book away until you have read the summary.

No two authors ever have exactly the same plans. But there are certain similarities in the way most books are organized. Authors who write fiction usually tell a story from beginning to end. In factual books you will usually find an introduction, a body, and a conclusion.

Being an Active Reader

In order to truly understand what you read, you must be an active reader. Active readers keep their minds on what they are doing. As they read, they are always thinking. Some readers almost have a conversation with the author. They ask such questions as "Does this agree with what my teacher said in class?" "Is this the only solution to the problem?" and "Have I ever had an experience like this?"

Some things that you can do to become a more active reader are listed below. Try them in your reading for school and even in your reading for pleasure.

1. Underline the main ideas. Even if you rent your textbooks, you can usually make light pencil marks that you can erase later. If you are really having trouble in a class, it may be worthwhile to find out if you can buy your textbook. You can then mark that book in whatever way seems best for your purposes.

2. Invent a code. You should avoid underlining details. But you should identify them and pay attention to the important ones. The best solution is to develop your own code to give yourself clues. You can then use

your code to identify different kinds of details. You can also make notes so that later you will be able to find information that was confusing or seemed especially important. Here are some codes that you may find helpful:

a. Put a circle around key words or unfamiliar words.

b. Put a single line in the margin for a paragraph that summarizes a section.

c. Put a double line in the margin for a major summary.

d. Put a star beside each example of the main ideas you have underlined.

You may want to put letters in the margin to stand for different things, like the initials of a person being discussed in the text or an abbreviation for a concept where it is defined or described. That way, if you need to write about something that you have read, or talk about it in class, or review it for an exam, you can just run your eye down the margin and find the right sections. You should also use brief notes. Just a word or two, like "causes of war," will summarize some details and actions so you can find them quickly.

3. Write a summary. You need not write in complete sentences or paragraphs, but you should jot down a summary of each section or chapter as you complete it. This summary may be placed either in the blank space that usually comes at the beginning of a chapter or in a separate notebook. If you have a good summary of each assignment, it will be easier for you to review later. However, the most valuable reasons for writing summaries are to make yourself think about what you are reading and to practice picking out the important information.

The only way to remember facts is to tie them to something you already know.

4. Tie information together. Keep in mind that the only way to remember facts is to tie them to something you already know. It also helps to try to think of how your own life might relate to the things you study in

school or how you might be able to use the information you are reading. You should also note any connection you find between one chapter and another or between subjects. For example, a fact you learn in American history might help you to understand a story you are reading in American literature.

Understanding Comes First

Comprehension skills are the most important of the reading skills. If you have to choose between working to improve your WPM rate and working to improve your understanding, choose to concentrate on understanding. It makes no difference how fast you read if you are not absorbing the information you need as you go. You will hurt your overall reading effectiveness if you concentrate on rate before comprehension.

Once you reach a comprehension level that makes you feel confident, though, reading faster certainly has advantages. If done right, a program to increase your reading speed should also work on improving your understanding of what you read. Keep in mind that both a good level of comprehension and a good WPM rate are necessary for effective reading.

V BUILDING A READING VOCABULARY

This section gives some pointers on how to increase your vocabulary, which will help you become a better reader.

malady

Cancer is a serious malady.

consistence (kən sis′təns), *n.* = consistency.
consistency (kən sis′tən sē), *n., pl.* **-cies**
1 a degree of firmness or stiffness: *Frosting for a cake must be of the right consistency to spread easily without dripping.* **b** *Figurative.* quality, condition: *Their friendship was of lasting consistency.* **2 a** firmness, stiffness. *The frosting retained its consistency.* **b** *Figurative.* substance, solidity: *The rumor persisted, daily acquiring consistency.* **3 a** keeping to the same principles and habits: *He showed no consistency of purpose. He did excellent work after that. A foolish consistency is the hobgoblin of little minds* (Emerson). **4** agreement or harmony among the parts, or elements of a thing. **5** *Obsolete.* gentle character. SYN: uniformity, regularity.

consistent (kən sis′tənt), *adj.* **1** keeping to the same principles and habits: *What a consistent person says or does today agrees with what he said or did yesterday.* **2** harmonious, in agreement; in accord: *Driving very fast on a rainy night is not consistent with safety. Too much noise is not consistent with comfort.* SYN: consonant, compatible. **3** *Mathematics.* having at least one common solution, as of two or more equations or inequalities. **4** *Rare.* holding together firmly; solid; coherent. —**consistently,** *adv.*

consistorial (kon′sis tôr′ē əl, -tōr′-), *adj.* of or having to do with a consistory.
consistory (kən sis′tər ē), *n., pl.* **-ries.** **1** a court of clergymen (ken sis′tər ē), *n., pl.* **-ries,** such as a senate of cardinals presided over by the pope having to do with a consistory. **2** a meeting in the Roman Catholic Church, a diocesan court bishop, or a governing board in some Reformed churches corresponding to the session of the Presbyterian Church, church council. **2** the meet- church council or court **3** the place of 32nd-degree *Poetic.* a meeting of the Roman emper- ies. **6** *Obsolete.* a north French consisto- [< Latin *consistōrium* < *sistere,* see etym. under

Building a Reading Vocabulary

Your success in school is related to the size and quality of your vocabulary. Students with the best vocabularies usually do best in school. Your vocabulary is all the words you know and use. You have two different kinds of vocabularies. Your smallest vocabulary is the one you use when you speak or write. Your largest vocabulary is made up of the words you use to read or listen.

Since this book is about reading skills, this section is devoted to building your reading vocabulary. When you increase this vocabulary, both your reading rate and your comprehension will improve. At the same time, you will also increase your speaking, writing, and listening vocabularies.

It takes effort to improve your reading vocabulary. The more you work on increasing your vocabulary, the better your reading will become. You need to build an attitude of curiosity about words. And you must develop the habit of really looking at words. In this section you will find a number of suggestions that will help you become more word conscious.

Finally, you should continue to build your vocabulary beyond your days in school. By learning and practicing techniques of vocabulary development, you will acquire a habit that will pay you rich dividends for the rest of your life.

What Is Your Skill Level?

Before you begin to work on building your reading vocabulary, you will need to find out what your word-skill level is. To do this, get some paper and take the word quiz for your level in school. The correct answers are at the end of the section.

Upper Elementary Word Quiz

Complete each sentence by choosing the correct word from the choices given.

1. A DON'T WALK sign means you are _____ to cross the street.
   a. allowed   b. reminded   c. forbidden

2. The astronauts _____ from their capsule to the orbiting spaceship.
   a. rescued   b. transferred   c. separated

3. A person who does not know what to do should get _____.
   a. ready   b. confused   c. advice

4. The Pilgrims left England and formed a _____ in America.
   a. colony   b. nation   c. territory

5. The subject matter of a book arranged alphabetically is called the _____.
   a. preface   b. contents   c. index

6. In the word *submarine, sub* is a _____.
   a. suffix   b. root   c. prefix

7. An _____ machine works by itself.
   a. oiled   b. automatic   c. operated

8. The letters *D, K,* and *T* are called _____.
   a. abbreviations   b. consonants   c. vowels

9. It is hard to walk on ice because there is little _____ between your feet and the ice.
   a. friction   b. gravity   c. contact

10. A _____ is a person from another country.
    a. native   b. foreigner   c. citizen

Junior High Word Quiz

Complete each sentence by choosing the correct word from the choices given.

1. A dispatch is an official _____.
   a. message   b. command   c. speech

2. A person who feels great bliss or joy is _____.
   a. romantic   b. in ecstasy   c. in a trance

3. To sew in designs on cloth is to _____ the cloth.
   a. knit   b. embroider   c. crochet

4. If you try hard, you are _____ yourself.
   a. exerting   b. forcing   c. overtaxing

5. Anthropology means _____.
   a. love of mankind   b. study of mankind
   c. having human form

6. When she decided not to take the plane, she _____
   her reservation.
   a. requested   b. made   c. canceled

7. A decade is _____.
   a. an athletic event   b. a geometric figure
   c. a 10-year period

8. Money paid out is called _____.
   a. credits   b. receipts   c. expenditures

9. A sudden desire to do something is an _____.
   a. impulse   b. impact   c. instigation

10. If a dead relative leaves you his house, you _____
    it.
    a. occupy   b. annex   c. inherit

High School Word Quiz

Complete each sentence by choosing the correct word
from the choices given.

1. _____ speeds up your heartbeat.
   a. Anesthesia   b. Analgesic   c. Adrenalin

2. _____ nerves deal with the sense of hearing.
   a. Cerebral   b. Optic   c. Auditory

3. To give praise unwillingly is to _____ it.
   a. begrudge   b. withhold   c. retain

4. The _____ is the frame, wheels, machinery, and
   running gear of an automobile.
   a. body   b. chassis   c. assembly

5. A _____ statement is scornful.
   a. conflicting   b. contradicting   c. contemptuous

6. When a person says one thing and does another, it destroys his _____.
   a. credulity   b. credentials   c. credibility

7. The _____ carries out the provisions of a will.
   a. bequeather   b. recipient   c. executor

8. The chemical compound _____ is applied to the teeth to decrease decay.
   a. chlorine   b. fluoride   c. phosphate

9. The Washington Monument, a tall, single, four-sided stone, is an example of _____.
   a. an epitaph   b. a mausoleum   c. an obelisk

10. The word _____ means a long, adventurous journey.
    a. sojourn   b. wayfarer   c. odyssey

Your score on the word quiz indicates how much you need to work on building your reading vocabulary. Here is what your score shows about your vocabulary:

10–9	excellent
8–7	good
6	average
5 or less	below average

A score of 5 or more wrong means that you need to do a lot of work on building your reading vocabulary. Even if your vocabulary is excellent, you should try to increase it because the more words you know, the more ideas you can understand and share.

Vocabulary study is much more than just memorizing lists of words or looking up the meaning of words in a dictionary. It includes taking words apart, using context clues, finding synonyms and antonyms, classifying words into groups, using vocabulary cards, reading a lot, and playing word games.

Taking Words Apart

The quickest way to increase your vocabulary and improve your understanding of words is by learning key prefixes, suffixes, and roots. Once you know these, you can begin to take words apart and analyze them. Learning to take words apart helps to give your memory a boost. If you do not know the meaning of a whole word, you may know the meaning of one of its parts. This can give you some clue to the meaning of the entire word. For example, it is a simple matter to take apart a word such as *bicycle*. The prefix *bi* means *two,* and the word *cycle* means *wheel.* Have you noticed the use of the prefix *bi* in other words? When you *bisect* a line, how many parts do you cut it into? Notice the *bi* in *bisect*—*bi* (*two*) + *sect* (*cut*). Once you know what the prefix *bi* means, you have a head start on understanding such words as *biceps, bifocal, bilateral, biennial,* and *bicuspid.*

By learning important prefixes, suffixes, and roots, you can unlock the meaning of many unfamiliar words. For example, the root *cred* means *believe* or *trust.* Notice the root *cred* in the word *credit.* When a person buys *on credit,* the seller trusts him, or believes that he will pay later. Did you ever think of the ideas *trust* and *believe* as being part of the word *credit* before? Taking a word apart makes you word conscious.

By learning important prefixes, suffixes, and roots, you can unlock the meaning of many unfamiliar words.

Building Vocabulary with Prefixes

Prefix means *something placed before.* A prefix is a letter or group of letters that is placed at the beginning of a word. A prefix has meaning. You can use a prefix to unlock, or at least to begin to define, a good many words. For example, the prefix *anti* means *against* or *contrary.* When you see a word beginning with *anti,* you know immediately that you're dealing with something that is against or contrary to something else. Knowing the meaning of the prefix *anti,* can you recognize these words?

antiaircraft

antislavery

antiknock

antisubmarine

antitoxic

antimatter

Pre (as in *prefix*) means *before: prearrange, pre-Columbian, preschool, prehistoric. Ex,* meaning *out of* or *from,* is yet another common prefix: *exclaim, exhaust, exit.* In addition, there is *super,* which means *above* or *to place over* or *superior: supermarket, superhighway, supertanker, supersonic, superheat.* And there is *sub,* meaning *under* or *below: subcommittee, subconscious, subcontinent, subcontract, subdivide,* and *sublease.*

Lists of common prefixes can be found in many dictionaries, grammar books, and books about language and usage. Work to familiarize yourself with common prefixes. They are an important aid to vocabulary building.

Working with the Prefixes Super *and* Sub

The prefixes *super* and *sub* are opposites. Use the correct one to complete the following sentences:

1. A _____ marine goes under the ocean.
2. _____ sonic planes fly at less than the speed of sound.
3. Extrafine sugar is _____ fine.
4. _____ *terranean* means under the ground.
5. _____ normal temperature is below normal.
6. _____ natural powers are beyond the natural.

Prefixes That Show Greatness

The prefixes *mega, hyper, ultra, extra, macro,* and *multi* show greatness in size, number, and scope. Do you know what each of the following words means? Look up the ones you don't know in the dictionary.

1. megalopolis
2. hyperactivity
3. ultramodern
4. multifaceted
5. extraordinary
6. macroscopic

Number Prefixes

You can have a lot of fun and really increase your vocabulary if you use these number prefixes:

mono, uni (one)

dua, duo, bi, di (two)

tri (three)

quad, quart (four)

penta, pent (five)

sex, hex (six)

sept, hept (seven)

octo (eight)

novem, non (nine)

dec, deca (ten)

How many of the following words would you know without help from the dictionary? Notice that they all begin with one of the number prefixes listed above.

1. A unicorn is a mythical animal with one horn *(corn = horn)*.

2. A diphthong is two vowel sounds pronounced as one syllable *(phtong = sound)*.

3. Trifocals are glasses with three focuses *(foc = focus)*.

4. A quadrilateral figure has four sides *(lateral = side)*.

5. The Pentagon in Washington, D.C., is a five-angled, five-sided building *(gon = angle)*.

6. A sexcentenary is a 600-year anniversary *(centenary = a hundred years).*

7. Septennial is a double-duty word: it means *occurring every seven years;* it also means *lasting seven years (ennial = year).*

8. An octofoil is an ornamental figure with eight leaves *(foil = leaf).*

9. A *nonagon* is a nine-angled figure *(gon = angle).*

10. A millenium is a period of 1,000 years *(ennium = year).*

Building Vocabulary with Suffixes

As with prefixes, the more suffixes—or word endings—you know, the more word meanings you will have at your command. And this means a larger reading vocabulary.

You probably know that the suffix *ed* at the end of a verb such as *play* forms the past tense *played* and that *er* added to a noun such as *work* gives us *worker (one who works).* Another common and useful suffix is *less,* which means *without,* as in *fearless.* Add *less* to the following words and your vocabulary expands immediately:

help   child
wit   blame
thought   worth

The suffix *ish* means *like* or *somewhat like.* Think of the interesting words that you can make by adding *ish* to these words:

wolf   fool
sheep   girl
green   book

Scientists form many technical terms with the suffix *ology (the study of).* Can you figure out the meanings of these words?

oceanology   audiology
embryology   meteorology

The suffix *itis* is heard all the time in doctors' offices. *Itis* means disease or inflammation. What do you think the problem is if the doctor says you have:

bronchitis   neuritis
sinusitis   appendicitis

Suffixes that Show Smallness

The suffixes that follow express the idea of smallness:

ette   *ule*   *ling*   *ie*   *icle*
cule   *et*   *kin*   *let*

Do you know what these words mean?

duckling   particle
birdie   piglet
capsule   kitchenette
lambkin   gosling
ringlet   leaflet
streamlet   mannikin

Suffixes and Gender

You can change the gender (sex) of a word by adding the female gender suffixes *ine, ette,* and *ess.* Try changing the following words so that they describe females instead of males. A few spelling changes may be necessary.

Example: host   **Answer:** hostess

major   governor
lion   prince
tiger   waiter
hero   heir
actor   usher

The Final Suffix Self-Test

Which suffix does your experience tell you to add to the following words? Your choices are (a) *less,* (b) *ness,* or (c) *ment. Less* means *without,* and *ness* and *ment* mean *state of.* Check your answers at the end of the section.

Example: beard   **Answer:** beardless

1. prepared   6. blame
2. amaze   7. establish
3. color   8. commence
4. guilt   9. stain
5. assort   10. sick

Building Vocabulary with Word Roots

A root is something to which a prefix or suffix may be added. Often a root can also be a word in its own right. Many words belong to the same family because they are formed from the same root; thus the source of their meaning is the same. For example, many words dealing with writing are formed from *graph (write): paragraph, autograph, biography, stenographer, telegraph, graphite.* Because these words are not in sentences, you have no context clues to help you figure out what they mean. But you do have the root *graph,* which tells you that the words are related to writing. When you use such a root, you find meaning from inside the word itself.

The more roots you know the better. As the material you read becomes harder, you will notice that many of the new words you learn are formed from key roots. The names of inventions, discoveries in medicine, parts of the body, and technical words in all the sciences are often made up of roots from Greek or Latin. Here are some examples:

1. Latin *agri (field)* + Latin *cultura (cultivation)* = agriculture

2. Greek *tele (distant)* + Latin *visio (see)* = television

3. Latin *appendix (hang on)* + Greek *itis (inflammation)* = appendicitis

4. Greek *therme (heat)* + Greek *metron (measure)* = thermometer

5. Latin *aqua (water)* + Latin *ductus (lead)* = aqueduct

6. Latin *biblion (book)* + Greek *graphein (write)* = bibliography

7. Greek *ge (earth)* + Greek *logos (study of)* = geology

The Root Meter

The root *meter,* meaning *measure,* appears in many words. For example, a *speedometer* measures the speed of a car, while a *telemeter* measures the speed of a space rocket. The following lists contain many words with the root *meter*. Some of the words could be placed under more than one heading, but each is on only one list. How many of these words do you know? Check over the lists first, then read the explanation that follows.

Electricity	Mechanics
ohmmeter	odometer
voltmeter	speedometer
wavemeter	tachometer

Human body	Mathematics
calorimeter	centimeter
isometric	diameter
optometrist	geometry
pedometer	kilometer
thermometer	perimeter

Science	Poetry and fine arts
altimeter	metrical
barometer	metronome
spectrometer	symmetrical

Words with the root *meter* are very common in everyday life. A person comes to your house to read the *meters* that measure the amount of gas, water, and electricity that is being used. Many homes have *thermometers* that measure the amount of heat in a room.

In your math class you have learned about the *metric* system and all the words related to *meter,* such as *centimeter, kilometer, millimeter,* and *decameter.* In science you may have learned that an *altimeter* measures altitude and a *bathometer* measures the depth of water. An *anemometer* measures wind speed and a *barometer* measures air pressure. In addition, music teachers use *metronomes* to measure tempo, and art teachers speak of *symmetrical* forms. Even poetry deals with *meter,* which is the rhythm in a verse.

It is difficult to avoid using the root *meter.* An *optometrist* measures the power of your eyesight. There is a *dosimeter* to measure the dose of radiation to which you are exposed. And you even can keep in shape by doing *isometric* exercises.

Learning Word Roots

It is not so easy to acquire a working knowledge of roots. It means some memorization. But it is worth the effort because each root word you learn becomes a foundation on which you can build your vocabulary. Note how learning one root can be the key to many other useful words:

crat (rule)	**fid (faith)**
democratic	confide
aristocrat	fidelity
bureaucrat	infidel
autocratic	bona fide

hydr (water)	**vari (different)**
hydrant	various
hydrogen	variety
hydrophobia	varied
dehydrate	variable

Compound Words

Early in school you probably learned that two words could be joined to form a new word, called a compound word. For example:

blue   + bird = bluebird

butter + cup = buttercup

suit   + case = suitcase

When you see a new word, it may just be two familiar words that have been joined together. Can you recognize the two words that have been joined to make these compound words?

fatherland   greenback

steamship   mouthpiece

millstone   lawsuit

It is important to know that the English language grows mainly through the process of compounding. Therefore, you need to spend a lot of time practicing the use of meaningful roots, prefixes, and suffixes as compound forms of words.

Using Context Clues

Often you can guess the meaning of a word from its context.

There are many ways to learn words. One is by paying close attention to context clues in the sentences you read. Often you can guess the meaning of a word from its context—the sentence or paragraph in which the word appears. So many times a word is actually defined for you either directly or indirectly. Look at these examples:

An oyster is a sea animal with a soft body inside a hard, two-piece shell.

Schussing, skiing straight down a slope without turning or stopping, is the fastest form of skiing.

Do you know the drink of the gods? It's an ancient Greek word we still use today: nectar.

If a word is not defined, the way it is used in a sentence or paragraph can frequently give you a good clue to its meaning. Note how the context helps you understand the word *divert* in the following sentence:

The farmer dug ditches to divert the water flow of the stream through the dry field.

You receive clues about what *divert* means from the other words in the sentence. Obviously, the ditches are changing, or turning aside, the direction of the water's flow. So, without looking up the word, you can guess in this case that *divert* means *turn aside* or *change*.

Finding Synonyms and Antonyms

An important way to sharpen your vocabulary is to notice the likenesses and differences in words. A synonym is a word that means about the same as another word. For example, the word *little* has many synonyms, including *tiny, wee, small, miniature, dwarf,* and *elf.* The more difficult words *diminutive* and *pygmy* also mean *little.* Once you have learned the general meaning of a word, you can then concentrate on the differences. For example, even though *tiny* and *miniature* both mean *little,* the two words are not identical. Each has a separate meaning in addition to the meaning they have in common.

Use synonyms to learn difficult new words. It is much easier to remember *superstructure, pinnacle,* and *apex* once you know these three words are synonyms of *top.*

Use synonyms to learn difficult new words.

Another way to learn words is to think about their differences. Word pairs of opposite meaning include *up* and *down, wet* and *dry,* and *hot* and *cold.* Words of opposite meaning are antonyms. When you study antonyms, you begin to understand the relationship between words. If there is an *up,* there must be a *down.* If there is *light,* there must be *dark.* One idea does not exist without the other.

Therefore, when you learn a new word, it is a good idea to also learn its antonym. It will not take long, and one word is easier to remember when you pair it with another. Some examples of words and their antonyms are:

male—female

explode—implode

masculine—feminine

robust—frail

buck—doe

nutrition—malnutrition

Classifying Words into Groups

If you don't classify words, you may forget them.

If you don't classify words, you may forget them. Your mind can't receive and store every word separately. Attacking each new word as a separate task is too much work. You need to classify or put words in a particular category. That category might be made-up groups of related words. For example, it's far easier to learn *denominator* when you classify it with *numerator* and *fraction.* And to remember *electron,* it makes sense to classify it with the other parts of the atom—*proton, nucleus,* and *neutron.* You can also classify words with their synonyms and antonyms. You might learn *droll* as a synonym of *comical.* Or you might remember *dreary* as an antonym of *bright.*

Classify a word first in general terms. Put it with related words or with a synonym or antonym. Then learn the exact meaning of the word when the need arises. Classifying extends a word's usefulness and makes the word more flexible. It causes more ideas to become attached to the word.

Using Vocabulary Cards

Flashcards are the best tool for teaching yourself new words. They are especially useful in reviewing for tests. And just making flashcards helps you learn because you must write out each word and its meaning. On one side of the flashcard, put a word you would like to learn plus a sentence in which the word is used. (There is no point in learning the meaning of a word unless you also learn how the word is used.) On the other side of the card, write the meaning of the word. If the word has synonyms and antonyms, include them too.

Flashcards can be used very effectively with a friend. First, you can read the meaning while your friend gives the word. Then you can change places. If you each make a set of flashcards, you can increase your vocabulary even more.

Reading a Lot

If you don't read much, you won't meet many new words and your reading vocabulary will stay small. You will also get very little practice in taking words apart or figuring out what they mean from the rest of the sentence or paragraph.

The more you read, the more your vocabulary will grow. If you dislike reading because it is so difficult for you, then find materials that are easy to read. You don't need to practice reading only from textbooks, novels, or stories. You can also read billboards along the highway, menus in a restaurant, magazines, the comics, and the sports page. When you look at something, get in the habit of reading the print. And as you read, look for new words and information that you can use.

Playing Word Games

You will have fun increasing your vocabulary when you start playing word games. Games such as crossword puzzles, Scrabble, and Boggle force you to look closely at how a word is put together.

You might try to work anagrams. These are games in which one word is changed into another word by moving the letters. One example of an anagram is *are→ear.* Can you rearrange these simple words to find anagrams?

horse   north

groan   clasp

forest   blame

Finally, try making palindromes—a very challenging game. Palindromes are words or phrases that read the same backward or forward. Good examples would be *mom, dad, radar,* and *kayak.* Can you find the palindrome that completes each sentence that follows?

1. A girl's name that begins with *A* is A _____.
2. The Boy Scout did a good d _____.
3. The sun is overhead at n _____.
4. When eating a baby wears a b _____.
5. The color of her hair was r _____ than a strawberry.

Learning How to Increase Your Vocabulary

Besides using all the ways mentioned in this section to increase your vocabulary, don't forget two popular helpers—the dictionary and the word list. Some students think of the dictionary as merely a book with a list of words. They only use the dictionary to look up meanings and check spellings. They don't really know how helpful the dictionary can be in increasing the size of their vocabulary. They don't realize that the dictionary gives synonyms and antonyms for words and often uses words in sentences. In addition, the dictionary tells how words are pronounced and usually gives the history of the word.

Word lists assigned by your teacher or included in your textbooks can also help in increasing your vocabulary because they tell you the words that you should know.

Your reading vocabulary is an extremely important part of your ability to read. Yet vocabulary has a playful side as well as a serious side. Words help you to enjoy puns, jokes, riddles, and funny remarks. They also help you understand the important thoughts in the Declaration of Independence and the Gettysburg Address. How successful you are in increasing your vocabulary depends largely on how word conscious you become.

Answers

Upper Elementary Word Quiz

1.	c	6.	c
2.	b	7.	b
3.	c	8.	b
4.	a	9.	a
5.	c	10.	b

Junior High Word Quiz

1.	a	6.	c
2.	b	7.	c
3.	b	8.	c
4.	a	9.	a
5.	b	10.	c

High School Word Quiz

1.	c	6.	c
2.	c	7.	c
3.	a	8.	b
4.	b	9.	c
5.	c	10.	c

Final Suffix Self-Test

1.	b	6.	a
2.	c	7.	c
3.	a	8.	c
4.	a	9.	a
5.	c	10.	b

VI BECOMING A GREAT READER

Once you have mastered the basics of good reading, study the advanced skills in this section in order to become a great reader.

Becoming a Great Reader

B*y now you are well on your way to becoming a better reader. You have already learned how to increase your reading rate, comprehension, and vocabulary. This final section will teach you some advanced skills that will turn you from a good reader into a great reader. You will find out more about how to use the reading signals hidden in each passage; read illustrative materials; distinguish between fact and opinion and cause and effect; recognize comparisons, contrasts, and generalizations; and identify the author's point of view. You will also be told the secrets of reading textbooks, magazines, newspapers, and literature, as well as other materials that are just for fun. The purpose of this chapter is to fine-tune your reading skills.*

Using Reading Signals

Cities and states have signs posted everywhere to help people get where they are going. There are signs that tell what to do along the way: Stop, Speed Limit 25, Watch for Deer, Turn Lights On in Tunnel. There are also signs that give information: State Road 37, Dangerous Curves, School Zone, Railroad Crossing. If drivers ignore any of these signs, they may have trouble reaching their destination. It's the same story for readers. There are clues in every passage that tell how to read it and give information about what is going to happen next. If readers ignore these clues, they may become confused.

Noting the Punctuation

Punctuation marks are like traffic signals. Capital letters are green lights telling you to go—a sentence is beginning. Commas are yellow lights advising you to slow down. And a period is a red light demanding that you come to a complete stop. If you don't think that punctuation is important, try reading the following paragraph that has none:

the climbers rose at dawn and moved quickly up the slope to the base camp where did they go asked a reporter who was extremely upset to find that the party had moved out without him it was hard for him to reach the climbers who were moving fast in the morning hours the reporter hoped to join them when they stopped for a break did he meet them no he did not he climbed steadily however he was not skilled enough to overtake them

Reading the Signs

Besides punctuation, you will frequently find words that act like road signs in your reading. The most common of these signs is *and,* which tells you to keep going because more information of the same type is coming. Look at the message that *and* gives in this sentence:

Mark was dirty and tired and sore and hungry and sleepy after the 25-mile hike.

The four *and*'s in this sentence signal you to keep reading along at the same pace to find out more about how Mark felt after his hike. There are other word signs, such as *more, more than, also, in addition, furthermore, likewise,* and *moreover,* that give you the same information as *and.*

Word signs like *and* tell you that more of the same type of information is coming. However, another group of words, including *but, yet, in spite of, on the other hand, although, however, not,* and *nevertheless,* warn you that entirely different information is coming. These word signs are usually found at the beginning or in the middle of a sentence. Note how these words change the direction of information in these sentences:

Patty is an excellent student, yet she flunked the chemistry test last week. On the other hand, Al—a C student—passed the test. However, at the end of the semester Patty received an A in the course, but Al received a C.

Punctuation marks are like traffic signals.

There is yet another very important set of words that advise you to keep on reading because a summary or conclusion is coming up. Whenever you see words like *therefore, thus, finally, consequently,* or *in conclusion,* you are approaching material that sums up what you have been reading. See how the word *therefore* introduces the conclusion of the following paragraph:

> Patty received excellent grades on all of the chemistry tests but one, while Al received only one good grade. Therefore, Patty received the higher grade in the course.

As you read, watch carefully for punctuation marks and words that give you clues about what will happen next. Observing these clues will help you become a better reader.

Reading Illustrative Materials

Illustrative materials are all the graphs, tables, charts, diagrams, maps, and pictures that you come across as you read. They present important information and must be read. In fact, you will be at a serious disadvantage if you just skip over them. Many times illustrations are used because they explain the author's message far better than the printed word.

Many times illustrations are used because they explain the author's message far better than the printed word.

Tables

A table is a collection of information that has been organized into columns with headings. Many different types of information can be shown on a table. Tables can be very simple, like the one at the top of the following page, which a coach made to keep track of the number of baskets each player made.

As you can see, the coach wrote the players' names in the first column and tallied the number of baskets in the second column. Then, when the game was over, the coach used the third column to record the total number of baskets that each player made. The table made it easy for the coach to discover who made the least number of baskets and who made the most baskets.

Players	Tally of baskets	Total baskets
Dan	𝍸 𝍸	10
Amy	𝍸 𝍸 ||	12
Marc	𝍸 𝍸 𝍸 |||	18
Ilene	𝍸 |	6

Tables can be much more complicated than the one just shown. Note how many more lines and columns the following table has:

Recommended Daily Allowances of Chief Food Elements

		Weight					Vitamins						
	Age	In lbs.	In kg.	Calories	Protein (gm)	Calcium (mg)	Iron (mg)	A (I.U.)	C (mg)	D (I.U.)	Thia-mine (mg)	Ribo-flavin (mg)	Niacin (mg N.E.)
Children	1-3	28	13	1,300	23	800	15	2,000	40	400	0.7	0.8	9
	4-6	44	20	1,800	30	800	10	2,500	40	400	0,9	1.1	12
	7-10	66	30	2,400	36	800	10	3,300	40	400	1.2	1.2	16
Males	11-14	97	44	2,800	44	1,200	18	5,000	45	400	1.4	1.5	18
	15-18	134	61	3,000	54	1,200	18	5,000	45	400	1.5	1.8	20
	19-22	147	67	3,000	54	800	10	5,000	45	400	1.5	1.8	20
	23-50	154	70	2,700	56	800	10	5,000	45		1.4	1.6	18
	51+	154	70	2,400	56	800	10	5,000	45		1.2	1.5	16
Females	11-14	97	44	2,400	44	1,200	18	4,000	45	400	1.2	1.3	16
	15-18	119	54	2,100	48	1,200	18	4,000	45	400	1.1	1.4	14
	19-22	128	58	2,100	46	800	18	4,000	45	400	1.1	1.4	14
	23-50	128	58	2,000	46	800	18	4,000	45		1.0	1.2	13
	51+	128	58	1,800	46	800	10	4,000	45		1.0	1.1	12

Read this table to see if you can find the answers to the following questions:

1. How many calories should a female between the ages of 11 and 14 consume daily?

2. How much calcium should a child from 1 to 3 years old have each day?

3. What should be the average weight in pounds of a man from 23 to 50 years old?

4. Who needs 15 mg of iron every day?

5. Who should consume 2,800 calories daily?

6. Who needs 13 mg of niacin daily?

Graphs

Reading a graph is like reading a picture book: the graph tells a story in an easy-to-understand format.

Reading a graph is like reading a picture book: the graph tells a story in an easy-to-understand format. There are three kinds of graphs that you will come across most often in your reading—line, pictograph, and bar. Look at the different graphs. Even though each graph looks different, all have the same title and present the same information. All show the number of students who were present in a classroom on the first day of each of five different months.

Line Graphs

Line graphs are useful for showing numerical facts that change over a period of time. These simple graphs are made by drawing lines at right angles to each other. Look at the following line graph:

Number of Pupils Present

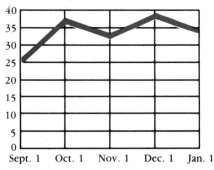

The vertical line is used to show the number of pupils present and the horizontal line gives the dates. Points on the drawing indicate how many pupils were present on each date listed. The points are connected by a line in the order that the dates appear. On which day were the most students in school? When were the fewest students in school?

Bar Graphs

As you can see from the following two graphs, the bars in a bar graph may be either vertical or horizontal and still show the same information:

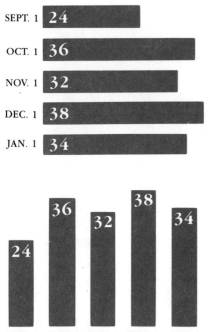

How many students were in school on November 1? On what day were 24 students in school? With just a glance at a bar graph, you can quickly see increases and decreases in quantity over a period of time.

Pictographs

The following graph is a pictograph:

SEP. 1   👤👤👤👤👤   👤👤👤👤👤   👤👤

OCT. 1   👤👤👤👤👤   👤👤👤👤👤   👤👤👤👤👤   👤👤👤

NOV. 1   👤👤👤👤👤   👤👤👤👤👤   👤👤👤👤👤   👤

DEC. 1   👤👤👤👤👤   👤👤👤👤👤   👤👤👤👤👤   👤👤👤👤

JAN. 1   👤👤👤👤👤   👤👤👤👤👤   👤👤👤👤👤   👤👤

Each symbol represents 2 pupils present

You will come across these graphs often when you are reading magazines and newspapers. In this case, the pictures are symbols that stand for students. But be careful—you must read the information at the bottom of the graph to find out that each symbol stands for two students. To discover the number of students who were in class on December 1, you need to count the figures and then multiply by 2. What is your answer? On what day were 38 students in class?

Circle Graphs

A circle graph is another type of commonly used graph. This type of graph gets its name from its shape. A circle graph makes it very easy to see what proportion something is of a whole. Read the following circle graph on the racial makeup of the U.S. population:

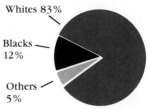

Whites 83%

Blacks — 12%

Others 5%

Note that the segments show the percentage of major racial groups and the combined percentage of all smaller groups.

More Illustrative Materials

Never skip reading anything because it isn't part of the main text. And when you study the maps, time lines, charts, and pictures on a page, be sure to read the words under them that explain exactly what they mean. For example, if you are reading a map, make sure to read what the scale is. In addition, when you look at pictures and charts, really study them. Try to find the details that the author wanted you to see. For example, notice the color of Napoleon's horse, what a Revolutionary War gun looked like, or that the ship has three sails.

To do anything well requires practice. Read tables, graphs, charts, and maps frequently. In fact, you should go out of your way to look for illustrative materials in newspapers, magazines, and textbooks. Once you find them, study them carefully. The more you read this kind of material, the easier and quicker it will become for you.

Distinguishing Between Fact and Opinion

Señor Gonzalez teaches the Spanish 2 class.

Señor Gonzalez, the Spanish teacher, is a very handsome man.

You have just read two sentences about a Spanish teacher. The first gives you facts, the second gives you an opinion. It is not always this easy to distinguish between fact and opinion. Yet when you are reading, it is quite important for you to be able to recognize this difference—especially when you are doing research or studying for a test.

A fact is a piece of information that can be proved. Study the following sentences. You could easily check that each of them states a fact.

Rocky won the Oscar for best picture in 1976.

Marco Polo visited China in the 13th century.

Alaska is the largest state in area.

An opinion is a person's own belief about something. An opinion may be held by just one person or it may be accepted by most people. Opinions can be based on facts, but they don't have to be. Opinions are often introduced by phrases such as *I think, we believe,* and *they feel.* And they often contain words like *best* and *worst.* Look at the sentences below. All are opinions.

> *Rocky* is the best movie that was ever filmed.
>
> I think that Marco Polo's greatest achievement was to introduce spices to Europe.
>
> Alaska is the state with the worst climate.

Two places in which you read both facts and opinions together are in magazines and newspapers. Can you distinguish between the facts and opinions in the following old news story?

> The *Titanic,* a British steamer of the White Star Line, sank on the night of April 14–15 after striking an iceberg. It was believed to be the safest ship afloat. The tragedy occurred about 1,600 miles northeast of New York City.
>
> The *Titanic* sighted the iceberg just before the crash, but too late to avoid it. The collision tore a 300-foot gash in its hull. The lifeboats took on less than half of the approximately 2,200 persons aboard. One of the survivors estimated that more than 1,500 passengers were dead.

You recognized the difference between fact and opinion if you classified all the sentences except the second one and the last one as facts.

Separating Cause and Effect

When you read, especially in social studies, you need to identify cause and effect.

Why do the swallows return to Capistrano every year? Why must everything that goes up come down? Why does it cost so much to buy a house in Hawaii? There is almost always a reason why things happen. And that reason is called the cause. What has happened is known as the effect.

When you read, especially in social studies, you need to identify cause and effect. For example, you will be expected to know the causes of such events as World War I, the bombing of Pearl Harbor, and the resignation of Richard Nixon. And you will also be expected to know the effects of the signing of the Declaration of Independence, the boycott of the 1980 Olympics, and the invention of the airplane.

In reading stories, you will find that you understand the plot better if you consider both the causes and the effects of the actions of the major characters. For example, what caused Huck Finn to run away and raft down the Mississippi River with Jim, and what were the effects of their leaving town? Whenever you read a mystery, you must focus very carefully on the cause and effect of each character's actions if you hope to solve the crime before the last page of the book.

To make sure that you understand the difference between cause and effect, think about all the possible causes and effects of the following events that might occur in your life:

1. You were absent from school last week.
    (Example: Cause—sickness, effect—lots of makeup work.)

2. You received a package in the mail.

3. You recently gained 10 pounds.

4. You lost the speech contest by one point.

5. You took a trip to Canada.

Recognizing Comparisons and Contrasts

By now you should begin to realize that top-notch readers are always thinking as they read. One thing that they think about is how people, places, things, and events are both alike and different. In other words they make comparisons and contrasts. When you compare, you mainly consider how things are alike. But you can also consider differences. When you contrast, you consider how things are different.

For example, if you were to compare Dorothy and the wizard in *The Wizard of Oz,* you could say that both were from another land and both wanted to leave Oz. On the other hand, in contrasting the two characters, you could bring out the different ways they arrived and left Oz as well as the different ways they helped the Tin Man, the Scarecrow, and the Lion.

Sometimes an author will make comparisons and contrasts for you. However, most often you will have to read the material and decide for yourself what the similarities and differences are.

Recognizing Generalizations

Generalizations can be very helpful because they sum up what you have been reading.

Authors often make broad sweeping statements called generalizations. When this happens, the author has actually drawn a conclusion for you. Generalizations can be very helpful because they sum up what you have been reading. Many generalizations are easy to recognize because they frequently include such words as *all, always,* and *never.* You will usually find generalizations in the last sentences of paragraphs. Sometimes they are written in boldface type in your textbooks in order to further catch your eye.

Generalizations are the rules in English—All sentences begin with a capital letter. They are the laws in science—For every action, there is an equal and opposite reaction. They are the broad general statements in your social studies textbooks—No war has ever had a single cause.

Textbook authors aren't the only ones to use generalizations. Authors of stories use generalizations to give you a better understanding of the characters, plot, and setting. For example, you might read generalizations like "Her hair was always well-groomed" or "Every person in the town was unhappy."

The problem with generalizations is that in some cases they are not true. Since generalizations are often based on just a few cases, they may not be true for all cases. So you must be very careful, especially when you read things like advertising claims, to make sure the generalizations are based on solid facts. Look at the following generalizations. Which ones do you think may not be true?

1. Blondes have more fun.
2. There are no good programs on television.
3. Earthquakes destroy property.
4. Everybody loves Mama Jo's fried chicken.
5. Snow is cold.

Knowing the Author

When you read a book, you need to become acquainted with the author. It helps, of course, to know about the author's childhood, education, and other works. But knowing an author really means finding out what the author's purpose is—the reason he or she wrote the book, story, or article you are reading. Once you know why an author has written something, you will be able to understand how the author has organized the material to reach that goal. Material is much easier to read when you know how it is organized.

Material is much easier to read when you know how it is organized.

There are clues that tell you what an author's purpose is. If you read a lot of *I*'s, *me*'s, and *my*'s, you know that the author is sharing personal experiences with you. This material is usually easy to read because you will not wish to remember all the details. If words like *think, believe,* or *feel* are added to the *I*'s, the author is writing his or her opinion on a subject. Sometimes the author will include a great many details. When this happens, the author is trying to give you information. You should then slow your reading rate and look for the main ideas and most important details.

Of course, authors have many other purposes for writing, such as proving that something is correct or incorrect, amusing readers, or presenting serious stories. Once you are in the habit of looking for an author's purpose, you should be able to find it rather quickly. Note how fast you can discover the purpose that each of the following authors had:

1. I'll never forget the summer afternoon I went out to the quarry when I was 16 years old. My friends and I planned to have a diving competition.
2. I think that all students should wear uniforms to school. I believe that this will help them concentrate on their studies.
3. The Deep Sea Drilling Project operates from a special ship called the *Glomar Challenger*. This ship has drilling gear and scientific laboratories. Advanced navigation and steering controls keep the vessel steady during drilling.

Reading Textbooks

Most of your reading at school involves textbooks. Whether you are reading a textbook for a health class, an English class, or any other class, there are certain things that you must do to get the most from your efforts.

Before you tackle any textbook for the first time, look it over, or survey it.

Before you tackle any textbook for the first time, look it over, or survey it. First, examine the material in the front of the book. Read the preface. It will tell you why the author wrote the book. Then read the introduction. It will tell you how to use the book and let you know if there are any other materials, such as study guides or workbooks, that can be used with the book. These aids can be very helpful if you have problems reading a textbook or find a course difficult. Also be sure to look over the table of contents. It will give you an overview of the book.

Next, investigate the material in the back of the book. See if there is a glossary of terms, an index to help you locate information quickly, and other aids, including maps, charts, tables, and formulas.

Finally, flip through the book to see how each chapter is organized. Be on the lookout for lists of words to be learned, summaries, and questions at the end of sections, chapters, and units. These are valuable helpers for improving your comprehension.

Studying with SQ3R

Once you are acquainted with a textbook, your plan for reading each chapter should be SQ3R. The letters and numbers stand for the steps that you will follow in using this method:

1. *Survey.* Read the headings to get an idea of the contents of the chapter. If there is a summary, read it as part of your survey.
2. *Question.* After reading the headings, turn them into questions. Now you have a purpose for your reading.
3. *Read.* Read to answer your questions. Read everything, including graphs, charts, and picture captions.
4. *Recite.* After you read a section, stop and write the answers to the questions for the section. Reread when it is necessary.
5. *Review.* Skim over the headings and recite your answers to the questions. Review after the first four steps and frequently before a test.

By using the SQ3R method, you should be able to read faster, pick out important points, and fix these points in your memory.

Reading Tips for Different Subjects

No matter what kind of a textbook you are reading, there are two things that you must always consider—rate and vocabulary. There is no one correct rate for reading textbooks. You need to adjust your rate to the purpose for which you are reading. As a general rule, read as fast as you can to achieve your purpose.

How well you can read a subject depends greatly on whether or not you know the special vocabulary that is required. When you meet new words that are essential to your success in a subject, put them on flashcards.

Social Studies

You must use your advanced reading skills when you read a social studies textbook. Pay particular attention to the differences between cause and effect and fact and opinion. Always read the illustrative material to "see" what the author is writing about. And finally, use the SQ3R method to study the material.

Science and Mathematics

To understand what you read in both science and mathematics, you must have a precise knowledge of these subjects' special vocabularies and symbols. Concentrate on learning the key words and symbols in these classes. Then use SQ3R to read the textbooks. When solving problems in either class, change the method slightly so that the Q stands for the questions "What is the problem?" and "What processes should I use to solve it?" The final R stands for rechecking your work.

Foreign Language

Read through stories in a foreign language at least once before you stop to look up words in a dictionary.

Read through stories in a foreign language at least once before you stop to look up words in a dictionary. Also get in the habit of using context clues to figure out the meanings of unfamiliar words instead of always depending on a dictionary. Be sure to make vocabulary flashcards and try to use them several times a week.

Reading Literature

In a broad sense, literature is everything that you will ever read. It includes comic books and pamphlets on voting, as well as the novels of Mark Twain and the plays of William Shakespeare.

In a narrower sense, there are various kinds of literature. For example, students read literature written in another language, such as French, German, or Italian, in their high school foreign language classes. Students also get the opportunity to study the writings of different peoples in their social studies or literature classes—for example, the literature of the American Indian. Students also study periods of literature, such as the literature of the 1800's. And there is literature about different subjects, such as the literature of science or the literature of homemaking.

But the word *literature,* in its strictest sense, means more than mere printed words. Literature is one of the fine arts. It goes back to the French phrase *belles-lettres,* which means *beautiful writing.* People understand the difference between this type of literature and comic books just as they understand the difference between professional baseball and a game of catch.

Literature has two main divisions: fiction and nonfiction. Fiction is writing that an author creates from imagination. Authors may include facts about real persons or events, but they combine these facts with imaginary situations. Most fiction is narrative writing, such as novels and short stories. Fiction also includes drama and poetry. Nonfiction is factual writing about real-life situations. The chief forms of nonfiction include the essay, history, biography, autobiography, and diary.

Reading for Pleasure

Throughout your school years you will usually read literature because it has been assigned to you. However, for many different reasons, literature is something that you will continue to read even after you leave school. Usually, the reason for reading literature is to gain pleasure. People read literature because they enjoy it.

Reading for pleasure may take various forms. People read just to pass the time or to escape their surroundings. Reading takes them away from themselves and into the worlds of other people. People read to gain information and knowledge. They read to find out about life in the Swiss Alps, on the Mississippi River, or at the South Pole. They find possible solutions to their problems when they meet people in books whose problems are like theirs. Through reading literature, people gain an understanding of situations that they would not otherwise understand.

Many people read simply for the enjoyment they get out of words. They find pleasure even in nonsense syllables, just as children enjoy the sound of "Ring-Around-a-Rosie" even though they may not know what the words mean. For example, read this silly verse aloud:

Ring-Around-a-Rosie

Ring-around-a-rosie,
A pocket full of posies;
One, two, three, And we all fall down!

Reading Creatively

No work of literature has wisdom or beauty by itself. The greatest poem ever written is only a printed sheet of paper until it has a reader. Writing becomes literature only when someone reads it. The reader helps create literature by reacting to the writer's thoughts, emotions, and beliefs.

A creative reader is always thinking about what an author wants to say and how it is said. A creative reader tries to figure out each twist and turn of the plot. The most important part of being a creative reader is to remember to bring your own life experiences and language to the experiences the writer puts on the printed page. You should measure the honesty of the writer's approach by your own ideas of truth. Creative reading leads to the deepest enjoyment of literature. Once you start reading creatively, books will take on a whole new meaning for you.

> *A creative reader is always thinking about what an author wants to say and how it is said.*

Poetry

Poetry is a type of literature in which the sound and meaning of language are combined to create ideas and feelings. When you read poetry, you should be able to experience the thoughts and feelings that the author is trying to express. Look for the rhyme in the poem. A rhyme occurs when the last word of one line has the same sound as the last word in another line. You should also feel the rhythm of the poem. Note how the flow of the words and phrases creates a pleasing sound. Once you sense the rhythm of the poem, the picture that the author is creating with words will become clearer and you will recognize it more easily.

Read the first part of "Break, Break, Break," a poem by the English poet Lord Tennyson that was first published in 1842:

Break, break, break,
On the cold gray stones, Oh Sea!
And I would that my tongue could utter
The thoughts that arise in me.

In these four lines, Tennyson tells of the connection between the sea and himself. The sea breaks up on the rocks much as the poet's thoughts seem to break up on his tongue before he can explain how he feels. This connection between the sea and the poet is reinforced by the fact that *sea* rhymes with *me*. In addition, the two lines about the sea and the two lines about the poet have the same 3-beat rhythm. Tennyson could have directly stated how he felt by writing something like "I wish I could tell you how rotten I feel today." By using poetry, however, Tennyson helped his readers both understand and feel how he felt. If you did not pick up any of Tennyson's feelings, try reading the lines of the poem aloud while paying careful attention to the rhythm.

Learning to Enjoy Poetry

Students usually get interested in poetry because of the sound and rhythm of a poem's words. As a young child you were read nursery rhymes. Read some nursery rhymes again. See if you remember the enjoyment and sense of rhythm that they gave you. Try these old favorites:

Jack and Jill

Jack and Jill went up the hill,
To fetch a pail of water;
Jack fell down and broke his crown,
And Jill came tumbling after.

Then up Jack got and home did trot,
As fast as he could caper.
He went to bed to mend his head
With vinegar and brown paper.

To Market, To Market

To market, to market,
To buy a fat pig,
Home again, home again,
Jiggety-jig.

To market, to market,
To buy a fat hog,
Home again, home again,
Jiggety-jog.

To market, to market,
To buy a plum bun,
Home again, home again,
Market is done.

Poetry's Appeal to Your Senses

Poets achieve effects by using words to create sensations in the reader's mind. Read the following lines from the poem "The Snow Man," by Wallace Stevens. See if you can identify the senses that Stevens is trying to appeal to.

One must have a mind of winter
To regard the frost and the boughs
Of the pinetrees crusted with snow;

And have been cold a long time
To behold the junipers shagged with ice,
The spruces rough in the distant glitter

Of the January sun; and not to think
Of any misery in the sound of the wind,
In the sound of a few leaves. . . .

If you identified the senses of touch and hearing, you are right. Stevens uses such phrases as "crusted with snow," "shagged with ice," and "rough in the distant glitter" to help the reader to sense the texture of things.

Magazines and Newspapers

You browse through magazines to see if there is anything you want to read. You glance through a newspaper to find out a score or the starting time of a movie. So often when you read magazines and newspapers you scan for particular information or skim until you find something interesting to read. Yet at other times you read magazines and newspapers for solid information.

If you are reading for information, remember that magazines and newspapers print both fact and opinion. Because different writers have different opinions, if you want to understand a controversial issue, be sure to read more than one magazine or newspaper. Try to become very familiar with several magazines and newspapers so that you know what their general views are. In this type of reading material, you will need to look very carefully at generalizations since they can be false.

Turning into a Great Reader

As you have read this book, you have learned how to improve your reading rate and comprehension and picked up the special skills that could help turn you into a great reader. However, you will not actually become a great reader unless you also become an active reader. To be an active reader, you must get acquainted with the author and find out what he or she is really trying to say. You may even go so far as to talk back to the author as you are reading. Being an active reader also means gaining an appreciation of words—liking their sounds and being curious about their parts. When you become an active reader, your reading skills will continue to grow as long as you live. And each year you will find that you enjoy reading more and that you are becoming a better reader.

Index